the 5 RULES *of* THOUGHT

ATRIA BOOKS   New York   London   Toronto   Sydney

the 5 RULES *of* THOUGHT

How to Use the Power of Your Mind

To Get What You Want

Mary T. Browne

ATRIA BOOKS
A Division of Simon & Schuster, Inc.
1230 Avenue of the Americas
New York, NY 10020

First Atria Books trade paperback edition October 2008

ATRIA BOOKS and colophon are trademarks of Simon & Schuster, Inc.

For information about special discounts for bulk purchases, please contact Simon & Schuster Special Sales at 1-800-456-6798 or business@simonandschuster.com.

Designed by Jaime Putorti
Background images © istockphoto.com

Manufactured in the United States of America

10   9   8   7   6   5   4   3   2   1

The Library of Congress has cataloged the hardcover edition as follows:

Browne, Mary T.
    The 5 rules of thought : how to use the power of your mind to get what you want / by Mary T. Browne.
        p. cm.
    Includes index.

    ISBN-13: 978-1-4165-3734-2 (alk. paper)
    ISBN-10:   1-4165-3734-1 (alk. paper)
    ISBN-13: 978-1-4165-3744-1 (pbk)
    ISBN-10:   1-4165-3744-9 (pbk)
    1. Thought and thinking. 2. Self-actualization (Psychology)
3. Future life. I. Title. II. Title: Five rules of thought.

BF441.B793 2007
131—dc22

                                                        2007014180

This book is dedicated to
Hubert Pototschnig

CONTENTS

We are what
we think

INTRODUCTION

*T*his book began with a thought. It existed as energy. My will molded the energy into ideas. The ideas were put into words. The book you now hold is a tangible example of the power of thought. There is nothing more powerful than thought. Everything in our lives is a result of our thinking.

For over twenty-five years I have been a professional psychic. My clients come from all walks of life and from all over the world. Many come to see me year after year. They come to me looking for answers to their questions. The most frequently asked questions concern health, money, love, or work. The men and women who come to me have one thing in common. They do not understand the power of thought and the effect it has on their lives.

Have you not met someone who looked up at a building and said, "I am going to own a building like that one day." And now they own one. Have you not heard someone say, "One day I will be president of my own company." And now they are. The answer is that these people saw clearly what they wanted, totally believed they could have it, and did whatever it took to get it. These people, whether aware of it or not, were using the power of thought.

The purpose of this book is to teach you how to think in order to get the things you want in your life. You will also find out how to tap into the Divine Force, which is waiting to help you. I have developed five rules of thought and the tools to help you implement them. They are the result of decades of studying the subject of thought and its effect on my clients and myself. The Rules are easier to follow when we first have an understanding of thought and an awareness of the great power that is available when our thoughts are guided by the Divine Force. This is why the book is structured to first explain thought, speech, the written word, and the Divine Force before focusing on the explanation of the 5 Rules and learning how to implement them. The 5 Rules of Thought are listed on page xiii. Study them and commit them to memory.

Thought is the most interesting subject imaginable, yet it appears to be the most ignored. People don't think about where their thoughts come from. They never stop to think about how thought is created. People think that thought is just there. It isn't. They do not understand that every aspect of their lives, health,

finances, love, work, and happiness are completely dependent upon their thoughts, and the actions that result from them. You choose your life by choosing your thoughts.

Start today to create your destiny. Read *The 5 Rules of Thought* and begin the most exciting journey of your life.

the 5 RULES *of* THOUGHT

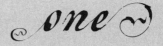

WHAT
IS THOUGHT?

A thought is an image projected into the ether. It is vibration. It is force and energy. It is creative power. It is spirit. It has color. It has sound. It has substance. Thoughts are completely alive. There is nothing more powerful than thought. You are what you think.

Every aspect of life is generated by thought. There are noble thoughts. There are mean thoughts. There are low thoughts. There are elevated thoughts. There are good thoughts. There are evil thoughts. All success and all failure are the results of our thoughts.

Everything you love is thought. Everything you hate is thought. Everything you feel is thought. Emotions are brought on by thought. Everything you see is materialized thought. Everything you hear is a sound wave composed of thought. In order to create anything, you must begin by seeing it in your mind. The thought is always first. Action is a direct result of thought.

You can get anything you want if you learn how to control your thoughts. In order to learn how to do so, it is important to understand that thought produces a dual effect: vibration and form.

▥ VIBRATION

A vibration is a wave of feeling that comes from the mind of the thinker. It expresses the character of a thought. For example, it may be kind, loving, generous, or angry. A vibration is also known as a thought wave.

Vibrations tend to impact the minds of others who are vibrating at a similar frequency. In other words, they cause the same kind of thoughts in the receiving minds as those sent by the original thinker. Thought acts as a magnet that attracts similar thought. Like attracts like.

Have you ever gone to a party and found yourself drawn toward a stranger for no apparent reason? It was not because of the person's looks or clothes. You had not spoken a word to that person. Yet there was something sublime. You could not put your finger on it,

but you were drawn toward this individual like a magnet to a refrigerator. The person's energy drew you in. The person had good vibrations. If you got to know that person, you'd discover an individual who had a fine character and was a nice person.

A vibration emanates as long as the thought is held. Every vibration is instantly followed by a form, which is a picture. This is known as a thought form.

■ FORM

Thought forms are mental pictures in the mind. If you think about an apple, the mind produces an image of an apple. If you think about a friend or a lover, the mind produces a picture of that person. If you are trying to write a novel, you will think about a concept. You will form ideas that bring the story alive. Once you have an idea, you can begin to write.

The intensity and the clarity of the thought determine the weight, power, and shape of the form. We have a million passing thoughts every day. These quickly come in and out of our minds. In the morning, the alarm sounds to wake us up. We think "alarm" and quickly turn it off. By then the thought is gone. You think, "Open the door." You open the door and then forget about it a moment later. You did not create a heavy form because you did not hold the thought, and you likely did not put much emotion behind it.

On the other hand, if you are really angry at someone and you keep holding the thought, it will intensify and take on a nasty form. This will then provoke an action. Maybe you will yell at that person, gossip, or start a fight. This type of thought form vibrates for a long time, even after you stopped thinking about it. Your actions were the direct result of the intensity and the duration of the thought form. Just because you say you are over your anger does not mean the results of the anger are gone. An angry thought form can live long after the action.

Thoughts create a form. The form becomes a picture. The picture may not be instantly apparent to the physical eye, but it is living in the "mental" plane. That is why thought forms are sometimes referred to as "elementals."

Thoughts that are directed toward someone move from the mind of the originator to the other person. A self-consumed thought will hang around the originator. This type of thought is completely about yourself or something you desire. For example, you have a strong desire for certain foods that are fattening and unhealthy.

You think intensely about these foods even though you are disciplining yourself not to eat them. This intensity produces a distinct type of thought form known as a "hanging" thought form. It is called hanging because it persists as long as you have the desire for something. You created a form that hangs over you even if you focus your mind on other matters. As soon as your mind is free, the hanging thought form will become apparent again. You will have an overwhelming urge to consume the foods you were trying to avoid. You will go to the bakery, buy a cake, and eat it, even if you are not hungry. You will call this temptation, but in fact you created this yourself. Nobody tempted you. You were the one who created this thought form. Strong thought forms always manifest. Therefore, it can be very difficult to stay on a diet. A clear thought, visualized and repeated will manifest itself in the physical world. Sometimes it may take time to manifest, but it will happen.

This is the same with addictions. Any addict will tell you how difficult it is to overcome an addiction. The physical craving can stop long before the mind lets go. The body will no longer crave them but people still cannot quit. The memory and desire for the addictive substance are still there. The person may stop indulging for a period of time, but the thought form is alive and waiting to be activated. In order to treat an addiction successfully the thought form must be changed. It must be rendered powerless. If the thought form hanging around the addicted person remains forceful, a relapse is inevitable. Thought is powerful. In order to avoid a relapse, a new even more powerful thought form must be created. The addict must learn to focus the mind on a clear, intense, detailed picture of being happy and free of the addiction. These positive mental pictures will help a great deal as one takes the active steps needed for recovery. These steps could include joining a specific program, consulting a medical expert, or even hospitalization. Any support system that works for the individual could be used.

Hanging thought forms aren't only connected to food, alcohol, and drugs. I have seen them hanging in the auras of clients who were obsessed with an ex-lover or spouse and could not get over these relationships. These types of obsessions can lead to mental and physical problems.

The age-old advice given by our grandmothers, "It takes time and someone else to help us put our past relationships to rest" is very potent. When we are able to replace the thought of our ex-love by the happy thoughts connected to a new love, the hanging thought

form starts loosening its hold on us. New thought forms are sent out from us to our new loves. I know it isn't easy to focus our thoughts on a happy future while we are involved in an unhappy personal situation. But change can be more easily enacted if we use the power of our minds to get rid of any hanging thought forms. I am not suggesting that you deny your feelings. Denial will only put the hanging thought forms out of your mind for short periods of time. The moment your mind is free, the hanging thought form will be apparent.

If you don't have a new love in your life, you must learn to see a clear picture in your mind's eye of yourself happy and in love. See this picture as many times a day as possible. Don't try to see a specific person whom you are in love with. Just see yourself happy and in love.

You can develop thought forms that will bring to you what you want. This is a skill. Like any skill, it takes desire, discipline, time, and effort. You have to acquire good habits of thought. This takes concentration and patience. You must see what you want clearly and learn to focus on it with intensity and faith. These are the first steps toward bringing your desire into form. You get what you think.

■ THE AURA

The aura is an invisible cloudlike substance that surrounds each of us. You have to be psychic to see it. It is composed of thoughts and the emotions that result from them. The aura emanates vibration and has color.

For example, the color rose springs from unselfish love. This love sends out a beautiful force. The colors in the aura reflect the character of a person's thought. There are certain stable colors in a person's aura. For example, intelligence produces shades of yellow. People have asked me, "What color is my aura?" They want to know what I see. There is a huge misconception that the aura is one specific color. Different thoughts produce different colors in the aura. In the course of a day, your aura could change colors twenty times.

For example, if you wake up in a terrible mood and act angry toward your family your aura will emit a red-orange hue. If you hold on to that awful emotion, the color will deepen until it is a raging fire red. This color vibrates in a way that attracts nothing but problems. But if you catch yourself and let go of the angry thought, replacing it with a calm, cheerful one, your aura will instantly change to a shade of blue-rose.

Your state of health, your mood, your talents, your

intelligence, and your character are clearly shown in the aura. One of the first things I see when a person comes for an appointment is the state of their overall health. This is indicated by color patterns in their aura. A person who is seriously ill will have shades of brown around the diseased parts of their body. If it is the beginning of a physical problem, a lighter brown, foglike substance will be visible. Happily, many times people return for an appointment and their illnesses have been cured. Their aura reflects their regained health. The brown has dissipated and has been replaced by a healthy shade of light green. A person of high intelligence will exude a yellow color around the forehead. Great talent radiates light purple in the aura.

We often see halos in paintings of saints. This is a light around their heads. The artists wanted to give us a feeling of their holiness. Spiritual souls think beautiful thoughts and these radiate glowing light and positive vibration. The halo is symbolic of the aura.

Judy

It was an insufferably hot Tuesday afternoon in July when Judy breathlessly arrived for her appointment. She entered my office and I knew it was going to be a difficult session. I could tell because I saw her beet-red aura. This color was not the result of the heat. It came from her negative thinking.

I asked her to give me a moment so that I could go into the other room to center myself. Taking a deep breath I returned and sat down, prepared for a difficult session.

"Judy, why are you so angry today?" I asked.

She lied to me and said, "I am not angry!"

"Not angry?" I interjected. "I am reading your aura and it's beet-red, which indicates anger and disdain. Do you want to tell me what's the matter or should I tell you that you just had a terrible fight with your husband?"

She was taken aback, paused, and then started to laugh. Her aura changed in an instant from red to a blue-green, showing relief. She began talking, and as she related the events of her day her aura changed again. It became a lighter shade of green showing me that she was very sad. She had found out that her husband had cheated on her and that he wanted a divorce. She needed advice on how to handle this situation. I saw there was no way to fix the marriage, and she should get out as soon as possible. Listening to me her aura changed to a shade of dull lilac that indicated fear. I calmed her with my prediction that she would get through this and find happiness sooner than she thought possible. I also helped her to admit that she had been miserable in this relationship for a very long time. By the time Judy left the session she was feeling balanced and her aura emitted a light blue color and a harmonious vibration.

A wave of emotion, negative or positive, creates a flush of color in the aura. Love will emit a shade of comforting pink or even white. Jealousy radiates an awful gray color. Kindness often appears as a wave of yellow-green. A clear bright yellow indicates intelligence. Several variations of flashing green expose a person who is lying.

Many people have told me they are upset because they cannot see auras. I explain that it's necessary to have psychic ability in order to see them. If you aren't

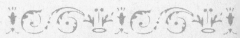

psychic, it is possible to become more aware of the way people's thoughts make you feel. When you are in the presence of someone who is kind and gentle you will feel warmth and comfort. A harsh, nasty person will leave you feeling cold and anxious. You don't have to see auras in order to be affected by the thoughts that create them. It's the same with your own thoughts. When you are thinking love, harmony, or kindness you will feel good. On the other hand anger, jealousy, bitterness, or revenge feels awful. The aura is a direct reflection of a person's thoughts and the emotions behind them. You don't have to see the aura in order to be aware of the influence it has.

■

You often hear it said about someone: "I just like them, they have a lovely aura," or "I could not stand him, his aura was repulsive." People react to the way that auras make them feel not because they see them. When I am asked by people: "How can I change my aura?" My answer is: "If you change your thought, you will change your aura."

■ HOW THOUGHT WORKS

Intense focus, which is concentration, gives thought power. You can get rich, find love, save your marriage, own your dream house, change your body, or just be happy, using the power of your mind.

Thought has to have an intermediary in order to have it do something. If you think you want cream in your coffee, you use your hand to pick up the creamer and pour it in. The hand is the intermediary for putting the thought into action. A machine does not work unless you turn it on. Thought, like the machine, needs a switch. Emotion is the switch. An idea without emotion is like a car without gasoline. It doesn't go anywhere. The minute you add fuel (the emotion) the thought starts to travel.

How many ideas have you had that never went anywhere? I am going to own my own business, be a lecturer, build a cabin, learn French, do the Tango, go back to school, or be a painter. All these ideas lacked the right emotion and the proper actions in order to realize them. Somehow the ball was dropped and the dream remained unfulfilled. The proper type and amount of emotion needed to execute the individual idea wasn't used. Emotion gives the idea energy. Thought needs emotion to make it happen.

Emotion does not mean emotional. When you are emotional your emotions are out of control. They control you, you do not control them. It becomes difficult to concentrate. Thinking becomes chaotic. Focus is lost. Energy is wasted. Some thoughts created by this chaos are: "I am too upset to work, to create, or to think." The emotions were meant to be tools to help us. They can vitalize and direct our thoughts.

When we learn to use the mind, we can override harmful emotions. The mind is stronger than the emotions. I am not suggesting that we suppress the emotions. This will boomerang and cause an eruption.

Bridget

Bridget was fuming on the inside. She was angry with her best friend, Heather. Bridget had been going through a difficult emotional time and she needed attention. Heather had always been a rock for Bridget. But Bridget got it into her head that

The mind is stronger
than the emotions

Heather had not been emotionally there for her. The problem was that Bridget never said a word to Heather about her feelings. She acted like everything was fine.

One day, out of the blue, Bridget blew up at Heather. She ranted about all the things that Heather had not done in the last six months. It seems that Heather was dating a new man and having the time of her life. This seemed to upset Bridget even more. Bridget's resentment erupted and the friendship ended.

We can learn to redirect the emotions. A strong will can take control and guide the emotions into a new habit of thinking and behaving. This new habit will enable you to get what you desire and maintain healthy relationships. Your mind will be the dominant factor in your thought process, not your emotions.

The emotions will act as motivators to action as they were meant to be. It is not just our emotions that get in our way. The emotions of other people can affect us as well. Any emotion can interfere with concentration. Concentration gives thought power. It is

impossible to get the things we want in life without concentration.

Do you know how many people over the years told me that they were going to write a book and never wrote one? They were not able to formulate their concept and shape it into book form. Sometimes the reason was simply that the idea was not good enough. Some gave up because they believed it had been done before. Overall the failure to execute the idea lay in their inability to use their thoughts properly. They were incapable of disciplining their thoughts and putting them into book form. These people had many excuses for why they had not finished what they set out to do.

Repeatedly, I have heard, "There was no time," or "I could not find a place where I would not be interrupted," or "I didn't know how to organize my thoughts." Successful people with a great desire to achieve something always find a way. When one door closes, they go to the next. They are passionate about getting things done. Their emotions do not hamper them. They don't waste time thinking about failure. They keep their focus on the project. The emotion behind the idea gave them added energy. The emotion could be patriotism, disdain, joy, or gratitude. Have you ever read the memoir of someone who survived cancer or some other fatal illness? The feelings of gratitude for their life and the desire to help others motivated them to write their story. Their emotions were helpful. Bottom line, successful people stayed focused. Their emotions were vital instruments to help center their ideas and bring them into form. Their emotions generated power.

■ BE CAREFUL OF WHAT YOU THINK

Thought brings to the thinker something of equal consistency. This means that it takes a strong thought to produce a strong form. This is how people become what they fear. They are alone because they constantly worry about being alone. They lose their jobs because they worry all the time that this will happen. They are broke because they obsess about having no money. The idea was in their mind and created a picture. The picture remained or was repeated over and over until it became a reality.

Andrew

Andrew is a tall, attractive, fifty-five-year-old, twice divorced businessman who was thinking about getting married again. He was dating Cheryl, a much younger woman who was a buyer for a department store. They had been introduced by Andrew's brother and sister-in-law. Everyone worried that Andrew was lonely. People always wanted to set him up with dates.

When Andrew came to see me he had been dating Cheryl for six months. He was convinced he was in

love. But I could see that this was not going to work out. I did not want to set the tone of our session by telling him that if he married Cheryl this relationship would fail. He'd already been twice divorced.

Sometimes I can see in the aura of clients that they are not able to take a direct psychic prediction. It would be too upsetting for them. In those cases I go slowly, allowing the person time to become confident that I have their best interest at heart. I first told Andrew the positive things that I saw in his present and future.

"But what about Cheryl?" he interjected into the conversation. He seemed desperate to know what I saw.

"Andrew, what's the hurry?" I asked.

"I am in love."

"Well, Andrew, weren't you in love the last two times you got married?"

He seemed surprised that I knew that. But he was delighted as well. The emphasis of my counseling is not based on my ability to know things that I haven't been told by the client. But that is what people expect of me. It gives them confidence in my ability. And it's also fun.

Andrew reflected upon this and said: "I thought I was in love each time I got married."

"I don't think you were in love. I think you were just lonely. That's why you got married. I believe you are still lonely. I do not think that this is a good reason to enter into a marriage. It's normal to want to be in a relationship. But you should not choose a partner because your mind is focused on the terror of being alone."

Andrew was taken aback by what I said. Then he admitted: "Ever since I was a teenager, I worried I would end up old and alone. My uncle Bob ended up in a nursing home with no wife or children. My mother kept telling me that's what happens when you are not married."

"Andrew, you have held the picture in your mind of yourself being old and lonely for over forty years. You are making this a reality in your life. You may not realize it, but you are reproducing this picture over and over. You must replace it with a picture of yourself happy and in love. If you make a conscious effort to change the picture, you'll change your life. You create what you hold in your mind. The strongest picture held for the longest time manifests. You keep bringing relationships into your life that don't work because you see yourself as old and lonely."

I could see by his reaction that he understood.

"I never thought about it that way. But I think you

are right. My mother's words stayed with me. I am afraid of being alone, but I still think I am in love with Cheryl."

"Andrew, can you give it a year before you go ahead and get married? This will give you time to see if the love lasts. If you still feel you are in love after one year, go ahead and get married. In one year you will know if the third time is a charm or if it is three strikes and you are out."

Andrew could not stop laughing, and said he would wait a year. He would get engaged but would not get married for a year. I also reminded him that he must erase the picture of being lonely and old from his mind. He could do this by replacing that image with a picture of himself being happy and well cared for.

I explained that he needed to spend one conscious minute two times every day focusing on his new picture. It would be even better if he could focus longer. Whenever the image of old and lonely came into his mind, he must force himself to think of the opposite. It would take effort. Andrew aggreed to give it a try.

Andrew came back exactly one year later. He had not married Cheryl. He was not in love after all. The thought of being alone was not strong anymore. He was more confident and secure about himself. This radiated from him. He looked balanced and in greater harmony.

Dan

When I met Dan he was a thirty-year-old, tall, handsome, successful stockbroker, making close to a million dollars a year. You can imagine how surprised I was when he turned to me during a late-night dinner and said: "I am terrified that I will become a bag person."

"What? Are you nuts? Why would you think that?" I asked him.

"I don't know why. I just know that I worry all the time that I will be broke and homeless. I see myself with nothing, living in the streets."

"Dan, stop it. This is a very dangerous way to think. You don't seem to understand how your thoughts create your life."

"Tell me," he said with genuine interest.

I proceeded to explain. "Dan your thoughts create pictures in your mind and these pictures in time become realities. Some thoughts are passing thoughts. They have little effect because they are not strong enough to last. But a powerful thought repeated over and over, like your thought of being a 'bag person,' will become a

reality. See yourself continuing to be a great success in business. Don't keep picturing yourself losing everything or it could happen."

My advice fell on deaf ears. Every time I saw Dan I was amazed that he continued to voice his fear of becoming a bag person. I cautioned him again and again but to no avail. It became depressing to be around him. All his friends felt the same way. We could not stand being around his negativity.

I lost touch with Dan for ten years. One day out of the blue I got a phone call from a mutual friend. She told me that Dan had lost everything and was found barefoot and homeless. He'd been taken in by a shelter. The people at the shelter were kind to him. They fed him, gave him shoes, and guided him to a part-time job. The news saddened but did not surprise me. Dan shows us that it is possible to become that which we fear the most. Dan is an extreme example of "be careful of what you think."

Thoughts have form, color, sound, and vibration. As a psychic I can see and hear them. For example, a thought of envy emits a gray-brown murky color. It sounds like an out-of-tune piano key and sends out a repellent vibration. The vibration of a thought depends on the motivation of the thinker. Since there is no such thing as "good" envy, a thought of envy always vibrates negatively. But there are degrees of envy. The stronger the emotion behind the negative thought and the longer it is held, the worse the vibration becomes.

You do not have to be psychic in order to see the results of thought. For example, I saw an out-of-shape woman at the gym. She shot an envious glance at a fabulously fit young girl. The next second she stumbled and fell over a free weight. She was so involved in her jealousy that she did not watch where she was going. She had attracted the fall by her negative thought.

On the opposite end of the scale, the more selfless a thought, the more beautiful it vibrates. A thought of kindness vibrates with harmony and emanates a soft, warm, light pink color. Its sound reminds me of the purr of a kitten. This type of thought attracts goodness into your life. I observed a woman in a playground who was comforting a child who had fallen. Within seconds the crying child became calm and began to smile. The little boy threw his arms around her neck and kissed her on her cheek. I could see from the shade of light pink in her aura that she was exceptionally kind. From the smile on her face as she hugged the child, I could see that she was feeling the happy effect of her loving thoughts.

■ LEARN TO OBSERVE

Most people do not take time to observe their thoughts. It never occurred to them to do this. No one ever told them they should do this, much less taught them how. It takes a conscious effort to make yourself stop and look at your thinking.

Margie

Margie's divorce seemed inevitable. She was angry and critical of her husband. He could not please her. She badgered him relentlessly until he reached a breaking point.

Arriving for her appointment with me dressed head to toe in couture fashion, she threw her brand new Chanel bag on the couch and sighed with a sound that was almost a hiss. She had the look of someone who has a personal trainer, very thin but fit. Every detail in her dress was perfect. Her scarf was wrapped around her neck and tied with a flair that only a stylist or a French woman, trained in the art of scarf-tying, could execute. She was all in black and white because this combination was "in." Her shoes and purse matched perfectly, and complemented the rest of her outfit.

Margie's hair, makeup, and nails looked as if she'd just left the beauty salon. It was unfortunate that she had no clue that she needed to get her inner self beautified like her outer self. Her thoughts were creating forms that looked dreadful. She was a mental mess.

"Why are you so angry with Ben?" I asked.

"How do you know his name?" She appeared startled.

"That's what I do for a living," I kidded.

She smiled for a second and then she began her tirade. "He drives me crazy. He is selfish, lazy, and critical. He never listens. He treats everyone nice except me. I just had another fight with him on the phone. He was so rude that I hung up on him. I could wring his neck. He is a monster. I hate him."

She was possessed by an irrational anger. I perceived that her anger was rooted in deep hurt. This anger shielded her true feelings. I felt pity for her. All the money in the world would not buy her the happiness she was seeking. This could only be gotten through a conscious change in her thinking. The marriage could not survive if they kept up this negativity for much longer.

The only way to save the marriage was to change the picture of their relationship that she held in her

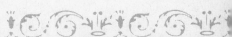

mind. She was seeing nothing good when she pictured her husband Ben. Her thoughts were radiating anger and disgust every time she allowed the image of Ben to flow through her mind. Her words precisely reflected the irritability and disdain she felt for him.

I asked Margie to tell me something good about Ben. A good thought about Ben could start her on the road to right thinking. My request fell on deaf ears. She point-blank said, "There is nothing good to say about Ben." The die was cast. There was no way to save the marriage. The divorce is now in the works.

■ OTHER PEOPLE'S THOUGHTS

Most people allow thoughts to flow into their minds without any direction on their part. They are mediums for other people's thoughts. They can't originate a thought much less project it into a useful form. You will hear them repeating things they heard on television or the radio. They are happy to accept other people's views as their own. They seldom get what they want in their lives.

Many people are a synthesis of the thoughts of others. They do what other people do. They wear red

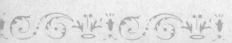

because everyone else is wearing red. Even if they look terrible in red, they never stop to think about it. Red is the current trend so they follow it. They read the latest bestseller because everybody is reading it. They repeat opinions that they hear on television. They follow the current diet fad, not because they decided it was the best nutrition for them, but because it seems the "cool" thing to do.

People who do not spend time disciplining their thinking are conduits for other people's thoughts. When we discipline our thoughts, we think for ourselves. We are conscious of the ideas and concepts we hold in our mind. We have to determine which thoughts and ideas are our own and which come from outside of us.

Wendy

Wendy had failed the bar exam two times. She was desperate. She wanted to know if I saw her passing the test. I got quiet and focused on her question. Then I saw a clear picture of her mother.

"Wendy, this might seem odd, but I see that your mother is interfering with your ability to pass this exam."

She started to cry. "My mother never approved of anything I did. She told me I was stupid. No matter what I did it was never good enough. I would get ninety-eight on a test and she would say that it should have been one hundred. I never cleaned my room properly. If I made cookies, I was not mixing the batter correctly. I did everything I could, but I could not please my mother. I got into law school. I was hoping my mother would tell me she was proud of me. Instead, she said I did not have the intellect to become a lawyer. She insisted I was wasting my time. I would never pass the bar. I also felt I didn't have any support from my father, who never disagreed with my mother. He never took my side. He did nothing. I loved my father, but I did not respect him. I wish he would have stood up for me. He died last year. I am an only child. Now it's just me and my mother. Now I have to take care of my mother."

"Wendy, what's the problem? Is your mother sick, or is she broke? I am sorry, but psychically I don't see any problems with your mother. It seems to me that your mother does a very good job of taking care of herself."

Wendy just stared at me. I observed that her aura, which had been vibrating a green-gray showing great irritation, moved to a color of green with blue spots showing me that she was perplexed.

"Wendy, I think you should focus on getting yourself taken care of and stop obsessing on getting your mother's approval. You think if you take care of her or do things for her, she finally will give you the approval you need. You need to finish law school, pass the bar exam, and become a lawyer. I see that happening if you can detach from your mother."

Wendy seemed offended in her confusion. So I continued, "Wendy, you don't understand thought. You are allowing your mother's critical and mean thoughts and words to mold your life. You have to make a forceful effort to free yourself from the bondage of your mother's mental grip. You are over twenty-one, you have a mind of your own, and you possess the most precious gift that the Divine Force has given us: You have free will. You can stop listening to your mother and start listening to your higher self."

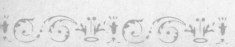

Wendy looked totally perplexed. "You can use your will to direct your thinking," I said. "You have got to stop your mind from allowing your mother's thoughts to come in. It may be necessary to stop communicating with her for a while. Focus your mind on seeing a picture of yourself getting your law degree. This is a place to start. Once you have your law degree, we can focus on the rest of your problems. One thing at a time must be your motto. Thoughts take on a life when you give them power. You have to refuse to allow the picture of yourself as a failure to live in your mind. You must replace that picture with that of being a happy, successful lawyer. Rome was not built in a day. It takes time. Your mind has gotten into the habit of responding to your mother's thoughts and words. It's time to grow up. Either you take control of your own life by taking control of your own thoughts or you are going to fail."

It was time to give her some tools to work with to change her thinking. I keep a legal pad on the coffee table for my clients to write things down.

"First of all, you must focus your mind on seeing yourself passing the bar. You have to have a clear picture of yourself passing on your next try. Add details that make your picture more real. For example, see yourself looking at the letter that states you passed the bar. See the celebration that follows the news. Do this exercise at least five times a day for two minutes at a time." I also suggested that she get a tutor to help her. She must study every day as if it were a full-time, nine-to-five job with overtime.

"Don't talk to your mother about the test. Once you pass the bar, your self-confidence will soar. You will have to continue training your mind to see pictures of success. In time, with persistence and determination, you will be able to release the false concept of yourself that your mother planted in your mind. This concept will dissolve and the real Wendy who sits in front of me today will emerge."

Wendy left the session motivated. She was determined to change her life and accomplish her goals. She passed the bar exam. It was difficult, but she pulled through. Her determination and hard work paid off. Her focus was more intense. She did not allow anything to divert her from her goal. This was a huge step forward in her life. She kept her mind on the test. She did everything to bring this about. She religiously did her visualization exercise. Wendy told me how much this visualization exercise helped her. It gave her added energy. She found that she enjoyed the minutes of concentration. They were relaxing as well as affirming. She felt a new strength. She was determined to remain vigilant with her thinking in the future.

Elsa

Elsa was depressed and did not know why. She is an only child. Her father had passed away in a Florida nursing home within the last year. Her eighty-eight-year-old mother is in the same nursing home. Elsa, who lives in Maine, has had to spend most of her time in Florida taking care of her parents. She never feels well in warm climates and has not had any time to herself.

I explained to her that she was being overwhelmed by thought forms of sickness and death. She spent every dinner with her mother and other residents, who constantly talked about their physical and emotional ailments. Many of the residents are lonely, so they are eager to tell Elsa all their problems.

"Elsa, you are taking on other people's thought forms. You must spend more time away in order to regain your balance. Other people's thoughts can live in buildings. Buildings can hold the vibration of the thoughts of those who live in them now and who had lived in them in the past. It is amazing how these vibrations can affect our own emotional state."

"I never thought about that. You are right. Even if I go to the shopping center or take a walk for an hour, I feel recharged."

She also had begun to take on physical symptoms of the people in the nursing home, though she had never been sick before. Elsa has always had a wonderful relationship with her parents and wanted to do whatever she could for them. But now she was overwhelmed by thoughts of illness and death. This was the root of her depression.

I again told Elsa she needed to get away from this environment to regain her balance. She would not be neglecting her mother by taking care of herself. She consequently went on a cruise. A few months later, I received a call from Elsa saying that she had a wonderful trip. She was feeling recharged and vowed to continue to take breaks in order to remain in balance as she continued to look after her mother.

Elsa was bombarded with sad thought forms. She missed her father. She felt love and concern for her mother and for all the others at the nursing home. It is normal to be sad when we lose a loved one. She needed

to grieve the loss of her father but she also needed to find some balance.

Many caregivers are not aware of the toll that the thoughts of all the people who surround them take. Places, as well as people, vibrate thought forms. It is important that we make our hospitals, nursing homes, and medical buildings as lovely as possible. Thoughts can envelop us and make it difficult to have perspective. It may seem too simple to advise Elsa to get away from it all. But it is effective. Changing scenery and energy changes our thinking. This change gives the nervous system a rest. This type of relaxation is life affirming and will result in a renewed sense of hope.

Observe your thoughts

■ RIGHT THINKING

Right thinking is a spiritual discipline that requires a conscious decision to be responsible for your thoughts. You must never allow yourself to dwell on a thought that is not positive, constructive, optimistic, or kind. Right thinking immediately sends positive force into your life. This force radiates from you and is a magnet for attracting good things.

What is a right thought? It is a thought of love, kindness, dignity, patience, success, harmony, or service. A right thought isn't selfish. Negative thinking is the opposite of this. Ill will, self-pity, greed, defeat, lack, hatred, prejudice, or revenge are examples of negative thoughts.

You should not pretend everything is all right when it is not. Problems will occur but they can be resolved through right thinking.

Theo

Theo felt defeated and wanted to know when his life would get better. Enveloped in self-pity, his aura was the color of mud. His voice was strident. It was obvious that his thinking was attracting nothing but failure. He had been fired by each of his last three clients. No one was returning his phone calls, nor could he get an appointment to see anyone. On top of it, his wife had left him and taken their two children with her.

I told him he had to take responsibility for his thinking. He looked at me as if I was speaking a foreign language. But he paid attention.

"Theo, stop pitying yourself. If you continue to call people thinking that they will not respond, then they won't respond. If you keep seeing a mental picture of yourself as a failure, you will be one."

"What should I do?" he asked.

"First you must see a picture in your mind of yourself successful with your work. You can make this picture any way you want. For example, see yourself smiling because of a positive response from someone who returned your phone call. See yourself busy with new clients. Keep seeing the picture of success in your work at least three times a day for at least two minutes. Let the picture go, and go on with your day. Proceed to do anything you can to make this picture a reality in your life. Keep calling potential clients, network with others in your industry, call former co-workers and ask for help. Do anything you can to bring work to you.

Once your business is stabilized, you will be able to focus on your personal life."

I stressed the need for sensitivity. Theo should talk to his wife when he was in a balanced and harmonious mood. This mood could only be achieved by thinking kind, loving, and nonjudgmental thoughts toward her. These thoughts would radiate a soothing pink color and this would have a healing effect.

I saw that his wife still loved him, but was not able to live with someone who was so negative and miserable. He left the session with a lot to think about. I have never heard from Theo again. I do hope he was able to change his life by changing his thinking.

■ YOU CAN ALTER YOUR FUTURE

The pictures you hold in your mind form the reality of your existence. If you change the picture you can alter your life. You have the power to do this.

A change in your attitude can influence your future for the better. Many people believe that the future is always predestined. It is not. Your future can be altered by your thoughts.

A decisive act can have a great influence on the

future. I predict a person's future according to the way he or she is thinking and acting. The thinking and the actions that result from this determine one's future. By changing their thinking they can alter the outcome.

One man, who came to see me, was in a dangerous state of stress. I saw that he could have a heart attack. He was under too much pressure from his current job. I pointed this out, and advised him to resign. This wasn't easy for him because he had a high-level position and earned a great deal of money. He left his job and took another one, though it was not as lucrative. But it wasn't a pressure cooker. He changed his destiny and his health.

You are what you think. Your accomplishments are the direct outcome of the way you think. Thoughts bring people, situations, and things into your life. Thoughts are like magnets. They attract similar thoughts. Every aspect of our lives is a direct result of thought.

■ POWER OF SPEECH

Speech is the process of putting thoughts into forms with language, sound, vibration, and energy. It has color and form, and vibrates with the emotion of the

speaker. Voice sets in motion waves of sound that radiate. These waves are picked up by anyone within hearing distance. Speech is a major device for bringing things into our lives.

Words awaken corresponding thoughts. Words are symbols of ideas. Speech should be an exact reflection of our thoughts. We should say exactly what we mean. Conflict arises when we think one thing and say another.

I was walking in Greenwich Village when someone yelled my name. I turned around and saw a woman I had known for a few years. She started telling me how wonderful I looked. Her aura showed me that she did not mean what she was saying. I could see the true thought forms emanating from her. They were repellent. I could not get away from her fast enough.

Have you ever been at a cocktail party or some social event when someone gave you a business card and said, "Call me. We need to get together." You called several times and left messages, but your phone calls weren't returned. You realized that person never intended to get together. Sometimes this type of behavior has little effect. But there are other times when it can have a great effect. Maybe you were going through a difficult time and needed help, and looked forward to talking to this person. However, the thoughtless disregard for your repeated phone calls and messages left you insulted and disheartened. That person's careless words, which did not reflect their thoughts, hurt you. People should not say things they do not mean.

Many times people make a verbal agreement and later disregard it. I know of two businessmen who made a verbal agreement for the rental of an office space. Several days later it turned out that one of the two, who was the property owner, wanted more money. He never discussed this and sneaked it into the lease agreement. When the prospective renter asked about the new price, which no longer reflected the verbal agreement, the owner simply said, "I changed my mind."

This type of behavior caused anger, resentment, and stress in the potential renter. When behavior of this type is repeated by many people in similar situations, it sends out waves of negativity. This has a tremendous effect not only on the people involved but on the world at large. Receptive people can pick up these vibrations and be influenced by them even if they are not conscious of it.

Words should be weighed. The tone should be considered. We should learn from the speech of others.

How do they sound? Are the words meaningful? Are they sincere? Do people do what they say?

I recently made an appointment to see a physician. I was surprised that I received a letter confirming the appointment. Underlined on the letter was the sentence that said: "Please be courteous enough to cancel your appointment at least forty-eight hours in advance."

Obviously, this physician was used to people not doing what they said they were going to do. This is a thoughtless disrespect for someone's time. It also could have affected another person who may have needed that appointment.

Speech takes energy. We should never say anything that does not have a positive purpose. We need to be vigilant about our speech and not allow ourselves to say things we do not mean. It takes energy to apologize for saying the "wrong thing." How many times have you heard someone say, "I'm sorry, I didn't mean to say that." This is repeated so often, it has become a modern-day mantra. How often have we had to say to ourselves, "I wish I would have kept my mouth shut"? Many times the damage has been done and "sorry" isn't good enough.

Take a moment to think about the people with whom you no longer talk. What is the reason for this?

Was it something they said to you? Something they said about you? Was it the way they said something? Could it be something they did not say? Is it possible that you offended them? As you reflect on the breakdown of communication, you should be able to acknowledge the root of it. The bottom line is that something caused this.

When we
think one thing
and say another,
conflict arises

Sarah and Luke

Sarah and Luke were married for ten years, but now no longer speak to each other. When they first met they could not have enough time for all the things they wanted to say to each other. Sarah told me that they talked until dawn on their first date. When I saw Sarah at a restaurant I asked her, "How is Luke?"

"I don't know. I have not spoken to him since our divorce."

"Sarah, what happened?" I asked.

"It started with little things. He would criticize the book I was reading, the dinner I prepared, the way I folded the laundry. Over time I began to feel that nothing I did could please him. He never gave me a compliment. He was always saying something that hurt my feelings. I began to get angry. We would argue over everything. Finally, we just had nothing to say to each other."

People tend to say things to their spouse or family members that they would not say to their friends or even strangers. We trust the people close to us to not abandon us over things we say. But this is a dangerous way to treat the people whom we say we love. Courtesy and thoughtfulness should always be part of our speech.

So many of our personal relationships are destroyed because of the way we speak to each other.

Prepare Your Speech

We often speak with no preparation that results in thoughtless words. But this is a mistake because those words have impact. Rude, abrupt, mean, harsh, nasty, or crude remarks have harmful effects. When combined with the speaker's tone of voice, they create discordant vibrations. These thoughtless words live long after they are spoken and affect everyone within hearing distance.

A boss who is rude or abrupt to his employees in the morning can set the tone of the office for the whole day. Likewise, an upbeat, happy greeting can get the staff in a positive frame of mind resulting in a productive workday.

I heard a woman scream at her teenage son in the grocery store. Her angry, strident words, "How stupid can you be," caused him to look like a deflated balloon. Everyone who heard her was affected. We felt lousy. Happily, there was a man standing by this deflated boy. He smiled and gave the boy a kind nod. This simple action from a stranger had an immediate effect. The boy was bolstered by this loving thought.

In this case a word was not needed. It was the thought that counted.

A seemingly casual compliment, such as "Your hair looks great" or "I love the color of your sweater," creates a lovely atmosphere. It makes us feel good. Notice what one kind word can do. It can give hope and courage to others.

Don't pass by someone at work who is obviously depressed or upset. Say something. You don't have to interfere in something that may not be any of your business. Just send a good thought and say, "Hello" or "Can I help you?" We should not withhold a sincere word of encouragement or help. These words vibrate with positive force and affect not only the people involved but others as well.

Every time we help someone we send a small blessing out into the atmosphere. This blessing helps us more than you can imagine. As we speak from a sincere desire to be kind and helpful we radiate glowing thought forms. Our auras brighten. These thoughts strengthen our own character. The stronger our character becomes the more control we will have over our lives. We all have the power to set the tone of our words before we talk. This takes a conscious effort on our part. We must become vigilant in our resolve to clean up our speech.

Unkind words can devastate people or cause them to be disheartened or offended. It is no accident that the phrase "think before you speak" is part of everyone's vernacular. Never waste words on cruel, mean, nasty, or negative chatter. These types of words produce bad energy. Bad energy brings bad things. Mistakes will be made and time will be wasted if we do not choose our words carefully. There are certain words that vibrate badly. Obscene words are never a good idea. They produce terrible thought forms and they vibrate like discordant music.

Roger

Roger decided to observe his own words for one day. He did this after I told him that he was rude, critical, and hurtful to people almost every time he spoke.

He was a good man, but I could not stand to hear the way he spoke to others. My words affected him. I had told him to pay attention to everything he said for twenty-four hours. For example, when he asks his secretary to get him something, he must be aware of the words he uses and the tone of his voice. Did he say "please" and "thank you"? He must be aware of how he

speaks to the waitress in the coffee shop, the doorman, the housekeeper, and anyone he encounters. He made himself do this. It wasn't an easy task.

Roger was shocked when he realized how he came across to others. He was like Scrooge when he saw the ghosts of Christmas past, present, and future all in the same night. Roger, like Scrooge, woke up and became a kind man. He began to think and speak with greater courtesy and sensibility.

Roger told me that he no longer feels like being nasty and critical. People who meet him now could never believe the way he used to behave. He worked hard on himself. He told me that by changing the way he spoke to others he felt good all the time. This good feeling made him very productive and attractive. Roger is now in love and his work is terrific. He feels like a new man. He is just being the best Roger that he can be. This goodness was always there but bad habits of speech became ingrained in him. He used his mind to make a swift change in his own behavior—once he was aware of the toll it was taking.

Tactful, precise speech is our goal. Wasted words are a misuse of vital force. This throws away power. Energy is a sacred commodity and should be preserved. When we squander our energy we don't have enough when we need it. Every word has an effect even if we don't see it right away. The only way to preserve our energy is to watch our words. Constant attention is required until our speech is in our control. We need to take time to speak clearly.

Careless speech is disrespectful to others. Angry words can make a whole home vibrate and feel charged with bad, negative energy. Lovely, clear, constructive words will make the speaker glow with radiant energy.

An eloquent speaker can sway an audience. Passions and emotions can be triggered by the tone of the speaker. An orator puts his mental concepts into words and brings tone and emotion to his delivery.

You don't even have to see a speaker to be affected by their words. Radio proves this: whether the speakers are political, educational, inspirational, healing, therapeutic, or entertaining, they all have power. Radio has an enormous influence on listeners. The voices can inspire you, calm you, excite you, make you angry, or help you.

Wasted words
throw away power

Thoughts made into speech project greater power than those left unsaid. Every word that we speak creates a form. So it is important not to speak lightly. Sometimes we monitor our words, but the tone of voice can give away our real feelings. Tone of voice has a powerful impact.

Emotions of fear, anger, disgust, rage, disdain, jealousy, and hatred put into words have a definite influence on us long after they've been spoken. They are toxic. Every emotional state has a corresponding physical state. In short, words can make you sick. How many of us have been shattered by harsh words or idle gossip?

On the other hand, think of the comfort that well-chosen words can give us. We should remember to tell people that we care about them. It only takes a moment to ask someone how they are feeling. Everyone loves to hear that they are doing a good job at work.

Who doesn't like to hear that they look nice? Words that express kindness and consideration vibrate with a harmonious feeling. They create beautiful forms and emit colors such as baby blue and soft green. Words

Focus on our thoughts
and speech
will easily flow

such as "beauty," "love," "sharing," "giving," "harmony," and "integrity" should be used as often as possible.

Speech is an important way that we bring our desires into form. A client of mine got a job because the boss liked the way he spoke. The way we ask for something has a great deal to do with getting it or not. If we focus our thoughts correctly, speech will flow easily. We will not have to struggle for the right words. The right words will come. It takes skill to find the right words to bring something into our lives.

Matthew

Matthew came to see me because his marriage was on the rocks. He was distraught and desperate and wanted me to tell him how to fix the problem. The first thing I saw about Matthew was that he was a serial liar. His aura was an awful shade of green.

I looked at him and said, "Matthew, you need to start telling the truth."

His aura then flushed red, denoting anger, and he snapped, "What do you mean?"

"I meant what I said," was my reply.

Matthew remained indignant throughout our session. He kept demanding that he never lied to his wife.

This, of course, was another lie. His inability to tell the truth cost him his marriage. Matthew kept getting caught telling lies. His wife would no longer believe a word he said and filed for divorce. His words were rendered powerless. Matthew could have saved his marriage if he could have learned to speak the truth.

You can only accomplish things that you want in your life by thinking and speaking in harmony. The universe is organized in harmony. If you think one thing but say something else you negate the thought. The thought loses power and you bring nothing to yourself. The thought will render the words ineffective. Think before you speak.

Speech is an expression of thought. Through speech we acquire things that we desire. We set the tone of our lives. Speech uses a great deal of energy. It is better to speak only when we have prepared what we want to say. Kind words send out benedictions and lovely vibrations. These words create beautiful forms that show in the aura. Critical, harsh, mean, and thoughtless words send out distorted forms. These cause disharmony to the speakers and to those who are forced to hear them.

You can't think kind and speak crass. This doesn't work. The thought will be negated by the form made by the words.

Speech can bring great things to the speaker. It sets vibrations in motion. These will bring like vibrations back to the speaker. Our character is shown in our words. We must form our speech like we form our thoughts—with clear intention. Clarity is the most important element in manifestation. This is true in thought and speech. You cannot separate your speech from your thoughts.

Kind words
send out
benedictions

■ POWER OF THE WRITTEN WORD

Thoughts formed into written words create denser forms in the mental body. Thoughts are molded into words by the imagination. The words of great writers are imprinted into the ether with such intensity and clarity that they continue vibrating long after the authors have died. These great writings live from one age to another. Time does not weaken the force of their expression. It seems clear that these writings possess an added vitality, something otherworldly, a spiritual vibration. These authors were able to connect to the creative power of the universe, the Divine Force. William Shakespeare, Charles Dickens, George Sand, and William Blake are examples of such writers.

Thoughts and ideas travel from the mind into physical tangible forms through the written word. Knowledge is passed on to us this way. I read somewhere about the most important individuals who contributed to civilization in the past thousand years. Number one on the list was Johannes Gutenberg, who invented the printing press in 1450. His invention gave permanence to the written word and made it available to a mass audience. We still have not recovered from the loss of the

Alexandrian libraries in Egypt. They contained 700,000 books, gathered from all over the world, and were written on parchment, papyrus, scrolls, and wood. There were no copies of any of these books. There are conflicting reports concerning the circumstances of the destruction of the libraries. It is generally acknowledged that there were three fires. The first happened in the time of Cleopatra and Julius Caesar, approximately 51 B.C., the second one, around A.D. 400, was ignited by a mob of fanatics who felt it was their duty to destroy pagan literature, and a third happened during the capture of Alexandria by Amrou in the 7th century. These books were reported to contain the knowledge of philosophy, mysticism, history, and literature; in short, the entire knowledge of antiquity.

Social upheavals, revolutions, and religious movements have been inspired by powerful written words. When words are put in writing, they can be read over and over again. Every time somebody reads them, pictures are created in the mind. The pictures formed in the thoughts of the readers are sent into the ether. They are then picked up by people of like minds. These people will be influenced as well. Over time, this can influence millions. The words become living thought forms. They increase in intensity as often as the words are read and re-read. The written word is powerful.

There would be no history without history books. Books document the times we live in and most important, the way we felt about people, places, and events. Written words, like spoken ones, are interpreted differently by different people. Someone who has never visited a specific location but has read about it does not perceive the description of it, in the same manner, as someone who has. When we read about a place, our minds create distinct images.

When I was a child, I lived a great deal of my life through books. Living in Cascade, Iowa, rarely traveling more than sixty miles in any direction, books opened my mind to the world beyond the Midwest. I first fell in love with New York through the escapades of Eloise at the Plaza. At the age of seven, I made a decision that I would live in New York City, and I do.

Memories fade, details are lost, events are changed, and emotions are forgotten, especially if you don't write them down. It's good to write something down while it is fresh in your mind. Writing things down can be an effective instrument for triggering the memory. Many people make to-do lists that help focus and prioritize. Energy can be conserved by writing down things we need to do and then doing them. Our mind needs to find ways to rid itself of chaotic thinking. Lists can help us do this. Any action that promotes focus of thought is productive. Focus gets results. Writing can help us focus.

Writing is another way to manifest things. When we write résumés and proposals that is what we are doing. Many times a job interview isn't granted if the person's writing doesn't make a good impression.

Writing our thoughts down is a way to structure our thinking. When we write a letter, we usually take more time to compose our thoughts than we do when we make a phone call. That is why people feel that letters are special. It is obvious that extra time was taken to form the message. Letters take on an added dimension when we keep them. They can live as a constant reminder of the way we felt. Letters are recorded history. Most biographers would confirm that without letters their work would be made more difficult.

In today's world, the Internet has profoundly affected the way we communicate and we use it for many things—business, shopping, dating, paying bills, or gossip. But e-mail does not vibrate the same way as written letters. Somehow the letters from Abigail Adams to her husband John don't vibrate the same way if they had corresponded with e-mail. There is a science called

graphology. Experts in this field can analyze a person's feelings and character through examining their handwriting. This cannot be done through typing. But e-mail is here to stay. It is a universal tool for communicating ideas. Therefore, we should treat e-mail with the same respect that we give pen and ink. There seems to be a general disregard for capitalization, punctuation, and spelling in e-mail correspondence. This probably has a lot to do with the pace of our lives. But it does reflect thoughtlessness, or even worse, a lack of respect. Many job applications are deleted without further consideration because of this. It pays to spend a little time thinking before typing.

I wonder how many e-dates were lost because of careless correspondence. You may have believed that the words on your computer could be erased and forgotten. Not so. How many people have gotten into trouble because something they deleted was retrieved?

Jocelyn and Victor

Jocelyn is divorcing Victor after twenty-three years of marriage. Jocelyn had believed they were happy in their marriage. They have three great kids. Two are off to college; one is still in high school. All are good students.

Victor traveled a lot, but Jocelyn accompanied him whenever possible.

One evening, six months earlier, Jocelyn borrowed Victor's laptop. Her computer had crashed in the middle of a project. Jocelyn did freelance design work and had a deadline. Victor was on a business trip and had left his laptop at home. Jocelyn had never used his computer because she did not need to, but this was an emergency. She turned Victor's computer on and realized she needed a password. She tried to reach Victor, but he did not answer his cell phone. Then she remembered that twelve years ago when they shared a home computer he had given her his password. She tried the old password and was surprised to see that it worked.

Jocelyn thought he'd get a kick out of the fact that she remembered the old password. To her surprise an instant message popped up. She clicked it on and started to read. "Hey, sexy, last night was great. Roses are my favorite. Love, Eva."

There were fourteen e-mails from Eva. Jocelyn was devastated. She waited until Victor came back from his trip and nailed him. As hard as he tried to make excuses, they fell on deaf ears. There was no way out of this for Victor but to tell the truth about his affair. He had completely forgotten that Jocelyn had ever had his password. And it was his habit to delete e-mails, but he had neglected to do this while he was out of town.

In the divorce proceedings, Victor had no chance to deny his affair. Jocelyn had made copies of the e-mails before Victor had time to delete them. Letters can be burned, documents can be shredded, but e-mails do not die. Even though e-mails have been deleted they can still be retrieved. Be careful what you write.

A client of mine put on her résumé that she was fluent in French and German. She had studied these for a short time in high school. She thought this was enough to merit a place on her résumé. She went to an interview for a job she really wanted. You can imagine her horror when the man started by conducting the interview in German. Suffice to say, she did not get the job. She changed her résumé and took the word "fluent" off and replaced it with "studied."

How many people didn't get a job because they had lied about their university degree or past job history? It's best to keep to the facts when you are writing. It will save a lot of time and embarrassment.

A sensitive person can pick up a letter and feel the attitude of the person who wrote it. This is an art known as psychometry. You don't have to be psychic to feel these emanations from the written page, merely sensitive and observant. Your handwriting can be analyzed by an expert and your character is shown in the way you write the letters.

Lawyers constantly warn us to be careful of what we put in writing. In real estate, contracts must be in writing in order to be valid. In divorce proceedings, compromising letters are sometimes used as damaging evidence. Love letters are potent statements of emotions. Your mother probably told you to wait twenty-four hours before you mail an emotional, angry letter. Most often when you have calmed down you don't send the letter.

The written word is more powerful than the spoken word because it possesses a grosser material tangible form. People don't usually read each other's thoughts. If you say something and regret it, you can withdraw it with an apology. It is easy to forget exactly what someone said. The written word is indelibly imprinted. Thoughts pass, spoken words are forgotten, but writing is permanent.

The written word can be creative and inspiring. It

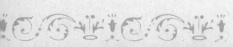

can teach, guide, instruct, entertain, and shift our consciousness. It has a huge effect on getting the things that we want. Good writing takes focus, patience, and persistence. Our writing is a reflection of our thinking. Be careful what you think. Be equally careful what you say. Be even more careful what you write.

*P*roper prayer
is always answered

THERE IS A DIVINE
FORCE WITHIN YOU

There is a Divine Force within each of us that can guide our lives. This Force is waiting to be acknowledged. We need to learn how to make use of this great power.

In order to feel this Force and direct it, we must be in a receptive state of mind. It takes aspiration and right thinking. The Divine Force responds to our will and does not work through adverse thinking. We must make a conscious effort to rid ourselves of harmful thoughts and emotions.

The first step you can take is to be happy with whatever you are doing. You may not like a certain task, but if you decide to do the job well and with enthusiasm you set up a positive force around yourself. This mind-set can carry you through many adverse circumstances. We must develop an attitude of reverence and devotion in our lives. The Divine Force does not lend itself to evil, selfish, destructive, revengeful, hateful, or criminal thoughts or behavior. These types of thoughts are manmade and are the opposite of elevated. They are the lowest forms of thought and will bring nothing but unhappiness, tragedy, and despair.

When we direct our thoughts toward the Divine Force, we begin to think and act in greater harmony. We allow our minds to be more flexible, more receptive to ideas. Faith is increased because we feel that we are not alone. We are helped and supported by this Spiritual Power. This makes difficult things seem easier and promotes a feeling of happiness. This Divine Guidance gives us better command of our thoughts. Negative emotions such as fear and anger fall by the wayside.

As we learn to use the Divine Force, we are able to feel in greater control of our lives. We find that we have greater focus. Our will is stronger and our thoughts are given clarity. This added clarity is very powerful. The thoughts vibrate faster and the will molds superior pictures in the mind. The Divine Force creates as well as supports. For example, I have been told many times about a miraculous power that helped people overcome an addiction. For years they had attempted to stop but their efforts failed. These people were able to utilize the Divine Force because they kept trying to conquer this dependence. Their will to stop, combined with faith and action, sent out powerful thought forms. These thoughts vibrated and connected to the Divine Force. The Force gave the thoughts the added power needed to succeed. Once they gave up the addictive substance, they reported that it was easy now to stay off it. The Divine Force makes everything easier.

Think about the countless cases of people who survive life and death situations. Many times they report a feeling of unearthly strength supporting them and leading them to safety. The Divine Force is creative and healing.

Musicians, painters, writers, and other artists often speak of divine inspiration. These people are tapping into the Divine Force whether they know it or not. The Divine Force works more effectively when we are conscious of it.

The Divine Force lives in all of us. A person does not need to know exactly how electricity works before turning on the lights. One must find the switch. The Divine Force is the switch waiting to be flipped. The Divine Force vibrates and surrounds everything at all times. The Divine Force cannot be seen except through its manifestations. All life is created by the Divine Force.

Constructive thoughts increase our faith and connect us more deeply with this Force.

When we allow the Divine Force to guide us, we are no longer confined by physical, emotional, or mental constraints. We are able to achieve our goals more easily because our thoughts and ideas produce more energy. It is impossible to fail if we think and act within the Divine Force.

The Divine Force demands action. In order to employ the Divine Force you have to show that you are doing everything possible. You cannot sit at home doing nothing. The Divine Force requires us to be responsible.

Cathy

Cathy, an attractive thirty-five-year-old, lived in a fantasy. She was broke and unable to pay her rent. But she believed that the Divine Force would solve all her problems. She spent hours each day praying for all her needs to be met. "I have faith that it will all work out," Cathy repeated like a mantra. She did not seek employment, knew no one who had funds to lend her, and did not try to get a loan from a bank. She just kept praying for money.

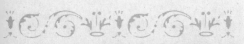

Eventually, Cathy was evicted from her apartment. A friend took her in, but was finding it difficult to have Cathy around. The friend, not knowing what to do, asked me to help. I agreed to try.

Cathy arrived at my office in a severe depression and looking as if she had not combed her hair for a week, and sat down without saying a word. I took a moment to compose myself. I was concerned that if she remained in this pessimistic state it would result in a tragedy. Taking a deep breath I asked her why she was so angry.

"Day after day I prayed to the Divine Force begging for help with my financial problems and nothing happened. I didn't get any money. I don't believe in anything anymore. I am devastated. Why am I not good enough to get help? What's wrong with me? Why was I rejected? I was told that prayer works. It doesn't."

I was struck silent for a moment. The magnitude of her ignorance about the Divine Force was staggering. "The Divine Force works with you," I said. "And through you but not without you. Your prayers should have been actions and not petitions."

"What does that mean?" she snapped.

"You could have used positive prayer. Positive prayer is active. Repeat 'I ask the Divine Force to guide

me, give me strength, faith, and fortitude.' This type of useful prayer will give you comfort and assistance. This spiritual help can guide you and compel you to take action to seek employment, apply for a loan, or get a roommate.

"Any of those actions would have reaped good results. Your aura would have been emanating positive energy because repeating a useful prayer always makes one feel better. Doing something makes one feel hopeful and this also shows in the aura. Opportunities for making money would have materialized. The Divine Force would have helped you to help yourself. Instead, you let the landlord evict you because you did nothing. You had an ongoing temper tantrum because you felt your prayers were not answered in the manner you had wanted them to be answered. And now you want everyone to feel sorry for you because your demands were not met.

"You kept demanding that the Divine Force give you what you wanted. Your idea of a prayer is petitioning a parental figure that will wave a magic wand and solve your problems. There is no parental figure and there are no magic wands. Give me, make me, show me, take me, I want, I need, I wish are useless and inappropriate and a waste of energy. They lead you nowhere.

"The Divine Force is not an external being that exists outside of us that we can petition for our wants and desires. It is part of us and resides in every living thing. It is the creator of not only our lives but of the universe and everything that exists within it. There can be no life, no order, and no possible harmony without the Divine Force behind it. Everything good in our lives is a result of the Divine Force.

"When we believe in the Divine Force, we make no mistakes. It is when we think outside of it that problems occur. For example, selfish, revengeful, destructive, sinister, hateful, envious, greedy thoughts are never done within the Divine Force. It does not lend itself to anything evil.

"Don't blame the Divine Force for your bad judgment and laziness. You must stop being angry at the Divine Force and start allowing the Divine Force to work through you. Take a moment for personal examination and you will realize that the Divine Force worked through your friend. She took you into her home and she got me to help you."

Cathy left that day with a great deal to think about, but she seemed a lot less depressed than when she arrived. Time would tell if she could straighten out her life. Positive prayer would help her if she used it. A year after this session Cathy's friend called me. She could not wait to tell me about Cathy. Cathy had gotten a job, moved to California, and was very happy.

Her friend explained how this happened. Cathy had come back to her after the session. She shared my explanation of positive prayer and the Divine Force. She also told her friend she realized she had been praying selfishly. At first her friend was skeptical, but she soon saw how Cathy's approach to life had changed. Cathy no longer expected things to be done for her. She did not pray for things she had not earned. She took things into her own hands and made them happen. It took her a few months to get her résumé together, and she did temporary work until she could find full-time employment. She kept the Divine Force in mind as she got her life together. She felt a special energy leading her and supporting her as she accomplished her goal of getting a good job and finally the financial security she had craved. Her friend had just received a beautiful "thank you" gift and a heartfelt letter of gratitude. This made her friend feel very good.

We can learn to become one with this Divine Force. To become one with this Force means to think and act at all times with Divine Guidance. It means allowing the Divine Force to work through us.

In order to feel this Force and direct it, we must be in a receptive state of mind. We must develop an attitude of reverence and devotion in our lives. We must live in harmony. The Divine Force does not lend itself to evil, selfish, destructive, revengeful, hateful, or criminal thought or behavior. These types of thoughts are manmade and are the opposite of elevated. They are the lowest forms of thought and will bring nothing but unhappiness, tragedy, and despair.

People ask me how they can connect to this Divine Force. It is easier for some people to utilize because they are used to asking a Higher Power for help. I will give you some of the best ways I have found to aid you to feel connected with the Divine Force.

*D*evelop an attitude
of reverence
and devotion

■ PROPER PRAYER

Proper prayer is not a petition. It is an acknowledgment of the Divine Force. It transmits a potent energy that is comparable to electricity. Proper prayer sets vibrations of a highly refined level into motion. These vibrations will produce an effective response.

Memorized prayers repeated by rote and those that ask for things we have not earned are useless. (Rote implies not being consciously aware of the meaning of the words that are repeated or chanted.) They merely constitute a misuse of vital force. The selfish "give me" prayers do not produce enough force to serve any real purpose. Prayers such as "Dear God, let me win the game, overcome my financial problems, find my true love" are prime examples of this. A prayer that asks to have your health restored when you have done nothing to promote good health is yet another example. In a proper prayer, you would ask that your ball team be given energy to play their best game. You would ask to be guided to a job that would solve financial difficulties. Instead of praying that Prince Charming will come into your life, pray for help to become a person that would attract someone like him. You would ask for strength and guidance in order to make the right choices to promote health.

Proper prayer promotes strength and courage. It is ennobling. When we think within the Divine Force, we protect ourselves. This creates a spiritual armor. We feel happier and with this feeling we find that our problems are solved with greater ease. Proper prayer does not have to be long, wordy, or poetic. It must come from the heart and the soul, the deepest parts of us.

When we pray fervently and with selfless motivation we reach the Divine Force, which answers us. The answers may come in many ways. Sometimes the answer will be immediate, other times not. But if you hold steady always keeping your mind on the Divine Force you will be answered.

Proper prayer helps us focus our lives. This focus will amaze you. You will feel blissful. Useful thoughts will come into your mind. These thoughts will help to resolve your problems faster. They are thoughts of a higher vibration and this vibration will bring to you amazing results.

Ellen

Ellen, an attractive forty-two-year-old successful money manager, was single and felt hopeless about finding true love. She arrived at my office, sat down, and immediately started complaining about God.

"I have been praying every day for over a year that God would send me a true love. Nothing has happened. No one has shown up. I have tried everything: the Internet, dating services, single parties, and the bar scene. I don't believe in God anymore."

I listened intently and when she finished I said, "Ellen, are you waiting for me to plead with you to forgive God for not giving you what you want?" She did not respond as she was still immersed in self-pity. I asked who taught her how to pray.

"Nobody taught me. I just ask for what I want."

"Have you always gotten it until now, Ellen?"

She paused and said, "Well, I never really prayed until now. People told me I should try prayer, so I did, but it didn't work."

"Ellen, it's useless to pray for something you have not earned. We always get what we deserve." I could see this made her really angry.

"I make $250,000 a year, live on the Upper East

Side in Manhattan, I stay in shape, I do everything right, somebody would be lucky to get me."

"Well, Ellen, that may well be the way you feel, but the reality is you don't have a love in your life. Stop blaming God and start taking personal responsibility. You must change the way you pray."

"Will that get me what I want?"

"Yes, Ellen, it will, but I have my doubts whether or not you can do it. Do not petition an external God who chooses whether or not you get something. God is the Divine Force that is within each and every one of us. This force appears to be dormant but in reality is waiting for you to set it free. Ask for strength and guidance to lead you into a happier personal life. This type of prayer alone will reap results."

Ellen took out a notebook and a pen and asked me to give her a prayer to write down. I gave her this: "I am one with the Divine Force. My strength and guidance comes from the Divine Force. All beauty, harmony, love, and peace result from thinking with the Divine Force."

I waited while Ellen wrote the prayer down. Once she finished writing, I continued my explanation: "These words may appear to be very simple but that is not the case. This is a potent, powerful prayer. You must sincerely mean every word as you say the prayer.

"Repeat this often throughout the day. You must do this in a respectful, reverent manner. When keeping your mind focused on the Divine Force, you radiate love and harmony. This will attract love and harmony to you."

Instead of starting your prayers with thoughts like "I want . . . give me . . . or I need . . ." think about the Divine Force and allow it to direct you.

When Ellen left that day I reflected on our session. I knew she was doubtful that my advice about prayer would help her. She could not conceive of praying without having a specific goal in mind. But I felt she would give it a try. What did she have to lose? She had tried everything else.

Occasionally, Ellen would come to mind. I would send her a positive, loving thought. I knew she could use all the help she could get. A year passed and to my surprise Ellen came back for another appointment. She walked in smiling, upbeat, and excited. Before I could say a word, she excitedly related her story. She had left my office a year ago feeling gypped. She thought she had not received her money's worth. But she told her mother about my advice for praying. Her mother told her to give it a try. So she did. It was difficult to get into the habit of proper praying. But she continued and in time it became easier. After several months she even felt comforted. It was no longer an effort to think about the Divine Force. It just felt good.

One afternoon she ran into an old college friend. Her friend asked her if she was involved with anyone. Ellen realized she had not even been thinking about a boyfriend. She had been feeling good about everything in her life. This friend asked her to come to a cocktail party. Ellen went to the party because she wanted to see her old friend again. She did not think about meeting men. This was a totally different Ellen. She talked to a lot of nice people at the party and enjoyed the time spent with her old friend. At ten o'clock, she thought about leaving because she had to be at work early the next day. As she was saying good-bye to the hostess, a man came into the party apologizing to the hostess for being so late. The hostess introduced him to Ellen, who immediately made him feel comfortable by saying "I, too, arrived late." They started talking, exchanged phone numbers, and from then on they became involved with each other.

Ellen's story is just one example of the workings of the Divine Force. She let go of her obsession to meet the right man. She used prayer as a focus. This calmed her and centered her. Without trying she had become much happier. This subtle change in Ellen attracted a lovely man into her life.

When you are centered and balanced you think differently. You are no longer desperate or impatient. You radiate an aura of beauty. This is a magnet for attracting good things into your life. Remember, proper prayer is always answered.

When a group of people together pray unselfishly, it is extremely helpful. For example, after Hurricane Katrina I witnessed televangelists asking thousands of people sitting in stadiums to bow their heads and pray for all the victims of this terrible natural disaster. This action sends a potent positive force to the victims. This force is received by the victims and it can serve to give comfort, strength, and hope. You may hear survivors relating how at the worst moment of terror and despair came a feeling out of nowhere that everything would be all right. I believe that a great deal of this feeling they experienced is the result of proper prayer being sent to them. The more selfless the motivation, the more powerful the prayer will be. Selfless motivation produces pure thought forms. These thought forms travel instantaneously. That is why the recipients will feel them immediately.

Before I understood the importance of prayer I

thought that people whose life work was prayer and contemplation were mere escapists. I thought they just do not want to face life. They would rather not deal with all the problems of living. I now realize how very wrong my thinking was. There are priests and nuns and monks who live in monasteries. They dedicate their lives to serving humanity through prayer and contemplation. This kind of prayer sends a powerful positive force onto the planet. Receptive people may pick up on this powerful force and be helped or supported by it. It can give people comfort. These prayers vibrate with the Divine Force and this helps the planet to stay in harmony.

Maria

Maria is a doctor. She told me that she asks the Divine Force to guide her as she works with her patients. This calms her and gives her focus. There are times that she feels overwhelmed because she is exhausted or saddened by her patients' problems and illnesses. Prayer helps her get through these times.

She told me that her prayers are always answered. Her belief in this is unwavering. This belief plays a big part in the success of her prayers. Maria is a very passionate woman. She does everything with incredible emotion.

Emotion causes her prayers to be answered faster. It gives her energy and clarity, which sends out a powerful plea. Her mind is not cluttered with useless thoughts. She focuses on her specific need and the need is met.

Maria says that it's easier for her to pray in church. Churches are quiet, beautiful places. She is not interrupted there. In the silence of the church, it is easier to hear the Divine Force. Maria reminds us to seek a place of comfort when we feel the need to pray, but it does not have to be a church.

Maria gave me this example of how one of her prayers was answered. She had been suffering from terrible headaches and was unable to find the cause. She asked the Divine Force to tell her what to do. A few days later, this happened. A workman came into her home to fix her fireplace and noticed the way Maria was sitting on her couch. He said, "Don't you get headaches when you sit that way?" Maria gave him a perplexed look. He said, "Look at the way your neck is leaning against the arm of the couch. I used to come home from work, fall asleep on my couch with my head lying in that same position and wake up with a headache. One day my wife noticed this. She got me to visit a physical therapist. The therapist showed me the proper way to hold my neck so I would not get headaches."

A light went on in Maria's head. The next day she went to see a colleague who was a physical therapist. This therapist confirmed that indeed her posture was causing stress on her neck, resulting in headaches. He made her aware of the way she had to sit and this, along with some physical therapy, resolved her headaches. Her prayer had been answered.

Exercise for Guidance

Find a quiet place where there are no distractions. Breathe deeply and start to relax. Allow the Divine Force to flow through your very being. As you feel this Force, let your feet relax, then your legs, your chest, through your arms, and into your hands. Relax your neck and your face. Let this Force flow through your mind. Keep breathing deeply. Now see a picture of what you desire. Spend a few minutes looking at this image. Ask the Divine Force to guide you. Keep looking at your picture. See it as if it existed. Allow the Divine Force to support you as you draw a more precise picture.

Go on with your life and do whatever you can to help this desire manifest. Stay open to all possibilities. Make certain that you are asking for something good, not something that will hurt others. Hurtful intent always brings something bad to you, be it now or later. Believe that your request will be fulfilled. The more frequently you pray the more effective it will be. The mind must be trained just like an athlete trains the body. Persistence is paramount.

Focus Exercise

Here is an exercise to help you focus. This is a very powerful method based on your breath. Visualize a soft color blue. Blue is the color of devotion. You must focus on the color blue. Take a deep breath and breathe in the color blue. As you exhale imagine that your breath is a beautiful shade of soft blue. Let this beautiful color fill your lungs. Now send this beautiful color out to the universe. Repeat this often and send this blue color out to the ether. This sends a very positive vibration and helps you focus your thoughts.

Concentration Exercise

Concentration is deeper focus. There is great power in concentration. Concentration molds thought into form. You must learn to concentrate if you want to control your thoughts. Holding a perfect thought is a form of prayer. Sit in a quiet place and close your eyes. Relax all your tension. Take a deep breath and exhale slowly. Take a second breath and once again exhale as slowly as you can. Now focus your mind on the word "harmony." The Divine Force is always in harmony. Everything good that comes to us is a result of harmony. To live in harmony is our sacred goal.

Hold the word "harmony" in your mind for two minutes. Set a timer if you must or learn to gauge the time. You may hold this longer but two minutes is the goal. Your mind may wander. Other thoughts may enter your mind. Don't worry. Just bring your thought back to the word "harmony." Keep concentrating and repeating the word "harmony" over and over in your mind until it builds strength. Remember, concentration of thought gives it power. When the two minutes are up, release this thought. Go on with your activities in harmony. Repeat this exercise at least twice a day. It will increase your concentration. It will make you more receptive to the Divine Force.

It is very important that you never hold an evil or a depressed thought. This will set vibrations in motion and cause injury to you or to others.

■ MEDITATION

Meditation teaches us to clear the mind. It is a discipline that teaches us to focus. When we meditate, we make a conscious effort to concentrate on a single thought, idea, or object.

First, no outside concerns must interfere with your thoughts. Of course, that is easier said than done. Our thoughts are like children, they must be put to rest in order to give meditation our full consideration. We must clear the mind in order to create space for the Divine Force to get in. Meditation takes a great deal of mental discipline. It's like cleaning a house full of clutter. There are layers of excess to do away with. This is time consuming and exhausting. You probably feel like quitting in the middle of the job. But think about how good it feels to have a clean house. Meditation clears the cluttered thoughts from our mind.

Meditation is an important step toward creative visualization. Before we can focus on a desired goal and bring it into our world we must learn to isolate a thought. The more intense our focus on a specific thought the faster something comes into form. Meditation teaches us to be single-minded.

Every religion, every spiritual teacher, every mystical book teaches that enlightenment cannot be achieved without meditation. It places you in a receptive state of mind. Deep meditation places you in a state between the physical world and the spirit world. "In the silence we hear the voice of the Divine Force."

Meditation Exercise on Happiness

Meditate on something that makes you happy. This could be your favorite meal or your favorite person. It could be a painting or a movie star. It could be a place. Everyone is different and everyone has something that makes them feel good.

Sit in a comfortable place and begin to relax your body. Take a deep breath and let it out slowly. Now start to think about the thing that makes you happy. Hold that picture in your mind. Keep looking at it. Focus. Enjoy this happy feeling. If your mind wanders, bring it back to your picture. Many people have a pet that gives them joy. Think about your pet. Focus. Look at the picture. Hold this for at least two minutes. Let it go and keep that good feeling radiating as you go on with your tasks.

This meditation is a great starter. It will begin to train the mind to focus on one thing. It can be very enjoyable. Do this every day until you can bring your picture up and hold it with no trouble. This may take a week or a month. The more often you do this the faster you will be able to focus your mind on one thing and one thing alone.

A few minutes a day spent thinking only of the Divine Force will have an enormous effect on us.

Find a place that makes you happy. It can be a room in your house, a garden, a park bench, or your favorite path to walk, or a lake; anywhere that makes you feel comfortable. Sit in a relaxed position; any position that works for you is the right one. Close your eyes, take a deep breath, and think the words "the Divine Force flows through me," or say quietly, "I am one with the Divine Force." Repeat these over and over until they are totally integrated into your very being. Do this simple exercise twice a day for forty days.

Everything that is good—health, wealth, true love, peace comes from thinking within the Divine Force. All positive thought comes from it. All problems in our lives result from thinking separate from it.

A few minutes a day
spent thinking only
of the Divine Force
will have an enormous
positive effect on us

■ CONTEMPLATION

Contemplation is a method of focusing the mind on a specific subject and exploring all aspects of it. Contemplation asks us to analyze something. There are different types of contemplation, which can be personal, universal, or spiritual. An example of universal would be world hunger. When we examine this, we consider all aspects of the problem. When did it start, where are the most affected areas, why aren't we doing more, what is the most direct way to get food to the hungry?

This type of scrutiny can be very useful in problem solving. It helps us make the right decision. Sometimes it is necessary to contemplate an issue for a short time. When we are deciding whether we want brown or black shoes, we contemplate this for a few moments. One might use this type of thinking to work out a relationship problem. For example, one party is neat and tidy; the other is messy and scattered. The first party may contemplate how to get their other half to clean up their mess.

When we are in love, we contemplate our love all the time. Where are they, what are they doing, how are they feeling, when will I see them, do they love me, and on and on. Take buying a car. One has to think about the type of car, sedan, four-door, two-door, six cylinder, eight cylinder, SUV, hatchback, station wagon, or convertible. After the type of car is decided, then you have to choose the manufacturer, the design, options, to lease or buy, the color, the cost to insure. Most people look at many cars, go back and look again, and in between contemplate what they are going to buy.

■

Contemplation on a higher level is an examination of a spiritual matter. This type of thinking leads to a deeper understanding of oneself. Contemplate this question: What can I do to become a better person? As you think about becoming a better person, ideas for improving yourself will come into your mind. You may clearly see what you have to do to achieve this. You may discover that a better person is kinder, more patient, nonjudgmental, helpful, generous, and loving. Once you identify what you need to improve, the necessary action can be taken. You will think, act, feel, and vibrate better. You will exude a more spiritual aura.

Contemplation of the Divine Force is powerful, potent, and sacred. You may ask, how do I contem-

Contemplate:

being a better person

plate the Divine force? What do I think about or examine? As with meditation, you must find a place that is comfortable and quiet. Once you have found a place, begin to see a picture of yourself looking very confident, fearless, healthy, and happy. Examine the picture. All happiness comes from thinking within the Divine Force.

Meditation focuses us on the Divine Force, and contemplation is seeing ourselves living within the Divine Force. The words contemplation and meditation are often interchanged. People think they mean the same thing. They do not. Contemplation is more active; meditation is more passive. When you contemplate, your focus moves to different aspects of the subject. Meditation demands that we concentrate our mind on one thing and one thing alone. They are both effective methods for helping us to feel our connection with the Divine Force.

Contemplation helps us to identify the root of many problems and makes it easier to solve them. For example, if you are easily provoked and can't figure out the reason, study your behavior. This will focus your mind on the problem. Once you are focused, you can then reflect on your attitude. You may see what you can do to change your behavior. Any change that occurs starts in our thinking. As we face our problems and discover solutions, our connection with the Divine Force strengthens. Our thoughts become more balanced and the actions that result from this bring happiness. When we think and act within the Divine Force, everything becomes easier.

Breathing in the Divine Force

Breath is life. Sit with your spine straight and your feet flat on the floor. Start by relaxing your body. Take a deep breath on a count of seven and as you inhale think, "I am one with the Divine Force." Hold this thought for the count of seven, and then slowly exhale to the count of seven again saying, "I am one with the Divine Force." Repeat this four times. The number seven is the number of creation. It is from the Divine Force that all is created.

The Divine Force is everywhere.

three

THE 5 RULES
OF THOUGHT

Here are the 5 Rules of Thought that must be followed in order to get anything you want. These rules always work if you follow them precisely.

These rules take effort. You must have a strong desire combined with discipline, concentration, patience, persistence, and faith. It takes practice. You are using your thoughts to bring your desires into the material world. What you think will become a material fact. Thought is the creative force in the universe. There is nothing more powerful.

These rules will teach you how to control your thoughts. Once you can control your thoughts, you will be able to bring your ideas into the material world. You will learn how to create the images that you hold in your mind.

These rules follow the laws of the universe. Thought is energy and vibration. Everything vibrates at a certain rate and speed. We attract everything to ourselves according to our vibration. There is an invisible influence known as the Divine Force directing us.

■ *Rule 1:*
YOU MUST DECIDE WHAT YOU WANT

Be exact and clear about what you want. You may want many things such as money, a new house, a promotion, a career change, a better body, a personal relationship, or marriage. But you must focus on them one at a time. This is absolutely essential. If you desire multiple things, you must choose which one you want the most. You may "want it all." Fine, but it can only be acquired by concentrating, separately, on each individual desire at a time.

You may ask why this is so important. The answer is, it takes energy to bring your desire into physical form. If you try to think of two things at the same time, each thought loses power. This power shortage will make it extremely difficult to bring either thought into being. Simply, the thoughts will be too weak to manifest.

Decisiveness focuses the mind and energizes our thoughts. We believe we can accomplish our goals. When we are decisive, we get things done. Decisive thoughts vibrate faster than indecisive ones. If you know where you want to go for dinner, you just go there. If you cannot make up your mind, you have wasted time and energy and probably wasted the energy and time of other people as well. How many times in the course of a day have you heard it said: "Make up your mind." It's either said to you or by you. Decisive thought results in direct action. We achieve our goals with the least amount of trouble. When you are indecisive, your thinking is chaotic. It's all over the place. Chaotic thinking is undisciplined, it lacks focus, and it does not go anywhere and wastes energy. You don't get anything done.

Fred

Fred works in an advertising agency as a graphic designer. He was given an assignment to create a package for a client's product. It should have taken him a few hours. He has done this type of assignment many times before. But his thinking was getting in the way. He would focus his mind on this project, but then he

remembered he did not call his mother. Then he thought, "I will do that later," and put his mind back on the project. Then he started to think about going out tonight. Should he make plans with his girlfriend? But he just saw her last night. Maybe he should call his friend Bill and have a bite to eat? "No, I'd better go to the gym, because I have not exercised in three days."

Then his thought goes back to the project. He focuses on color and thinks, "What color should the package be?" and he begins to scroll through the color chart. He sees "orange" and thinks about the orange miniskirt the bartender at the bistro near his apartment was wearing last Friday night. He thinks about asking her for a date. Then he goes back to the project and decides to make the package green. Then he remembers he forgot to water his plants. The phone rings. It's his friend Bill asking him if he wants to go to a football game on Saturday. He told him he was not sure about his plans for Saturday, but he would get back to Bill. He had to finish a project in the office. After he hung up the phone, he starts thinking about the football game and who is going to win.

Lost in thought about football, he was surprised to hear the receptionist say, "Good night, Fred. I will see you tomorrow." He looked at his watch and realized it was quitting time. He was nowhere near finished. He started thinking about the consequences. This caused his mind to start racing. He thought, "I will lose my job if I don't finish this. Maybe I can come in early and finish. No, that's too risky. I better stay until I get it done."

These thoughts wasted more time. Fred's chaotic thinking caused him additional delay. He had to stay until nine that evening to finish the project that should have taken two hours.

Chaotic thinking always causes delays or worse. Chaotic thinking interferes with getting what you want. This messy thinking lacks energy and produces thought forms that are not clearly defined. The only way to rid oneself of chaotic thinking is to focus. Fred needs to learn how to focus. With focused thought Fred would have quickly completed his project. Fred needed to think only of his project until it was finished.

Focus halts chaotic thinking. It is an act of will. When we focus, we command our mind to stay fixed on one thought or idea. Everything else is blocked out. Nothing exists except that one thought or idea. This is

a skill that takes effort and practice. Focus gives the thought power. When we focus on a thought or idea, we create a picture of it in our mind. The more intense our focus, the faster the thought vibrates and the clearer the picture becomes. Focus prepares us to concentrate. Intense focus is concentration. Concentration of thought is essential. The only way to get what you want is to focus.

The Book Exercise

In order to focus on getting what you want, you must learn how to isolate a thought. To do this exercise properly you will need ten minutes. You will need a kitchen timer or a watch that has an alarm or anything that lets you know when the ten minutes are up. You must choose a quiet, comfortable place.

Get a book and place it at eye level. Position the book so that when you are looking at it, you can clearly see it. Set the timer for ten minutes. Sit with your spine straight and with your feet flat on the floor. Close your eyes. Breathe deeply. Inhale and exhale. As you inhale feel your body tension leaving. Keep inhaling and exhaling as your body becomes more and more relaxed. Let go of all your problems. Just enjoy the fact that you have nothing else to do. This is your ten minutes. Once you feel relaxed, open your eyes and look at the book. Focus on the book. Nothing exists except the book. Your mind is thinking of the book and the book alone. Keep your mind on the book. If another thought enters your mind, go back to looking at the book. Think of nothing but the book. Continue looking at the book and the book alone. You are isolating a thought as you look at the book. The book is your isolated thought.

Your mind can think of only one thing at a time. We are learning how to remove a thought from our busy minds and make it the complete focus of everything. Keep forcing your mind to think of only the book until the timer goes off.

You will find that over time your mind will easily focus on the book and it will become like a meditation. When we focus our minds on one thing and one thing alone, we are magnetizing that one thought. We are energizing it and giving it extra mental force and power. This is the first step in manifestation. Once you are able to do this exercise for ten minutes, you are well on your way toward getting anything you want.

Not everyone knows what they want. Many people are completely clueless about what they want. They live their lives complaining that they are unhappy. They don't know what would make them happy. If you ask them what would make them happy, they draw a blank. This is tragic. It does not have to be that way. Anyone can learn to make a decision.

*Y*our mind can only
think of one thing at a time.

Shelly

I was sitting on an airplane on my way to Santa Fe. Exhausted from my hectic schedule, I was looking forward to the flight. This would give me time to read, reflect, and relax. A few minutes before departure a woman rushed in and found her seat next to me. Before she could buckle her seat belt, paying no attention to the fact that I was immersed in a book, she started talking to me. It was incredible. Barely taking a breath she told me her name and began to tell me that she was desperately unhappy. I listened as she went on and on about her miserable life. "I don't know what I want. I have never known what I wanted. I hate my job, but I can't think of anything else that I want to do. I don't like where I live, but I can't think of anywhere to move. I have an awful marriage, but I am afraid if I divorce I won't find a better husband. I don't know what to do."

Shelly is a perfect example of the type of person who is a prisoner of her own indecisiveness. The root of her problem was that she had no idea what she wanted. The world is full of people like Shelly. They simply can't decide what they want.

"Shelly, you are unhappy with many parts of your

120

life, but you must decide which parts can be changed most easily. You must focus on each of your problems separately in order to decide which problem can be resolved first. You must stop your mind from racing. You won't be able to find a peaceful solution until you learn to focus on that part of your life which you can do something about now."

This caused Shelly to think for a moment. "I don't know."

I realized that Shelly sadly could not make a decision. "Shelly, it seems to me if you could find work that is interesting, stimulating, and fulfilling you would feel happier about yourself. This would give you strength to decide about your home and your marriage. You have to focus on one thing at a time or you'll go crazy. Think about a new job, Shelly. Just make a picture in your mind going to a job that makes you happy."

Shelly seemed confused but said, "I will try to think about a job." Then she fell silent for the rest of the trip.

Whether you are like Shelly and you are indecisive or you don't know which desire you want the most, you

have to be able to focus the mind. When you focus you concentrate on an individual thought or idea. You have to prioritize. Shelly was unhappy with her job, her home, and her marriage.

I told Shelly to make a decision about her job. Resolving this would give her a feeling of self confidence. This self confidence would help to direct her mind toward solving the next problem. The bottom line is nothing gets solved unless you focus on one thing at a time. You have to decide what you want. Once you decide what you want you can focus.

Dennis

Dennis has been married for eighteen years. He had been dating his wife Kim since high school. They married soon after high school graduation and now have two teenage daughters.

Dennis came to see me because Kim had moved out of the house. He was desperate to get her back. He didn't realize that his thoughts were interfering with his desire. He believed that he was focused on what he wanted, yet as I observed him I could see anger, confusion, and disappointment in his aura. He was so upset that he could not focus on a specific thought for even a few seconds. For example, he told me he loved Kim, but in the next breath he said she was shallow. Then he would say she was beautiful but that her body could be in better shape. Then he would say, "I don't care about that. I just want her to come back."

For the next ten minutes, Dennis went on to tell me how betrayed he felt. He said his daughters were devastated by this and that it was completely Kim's fault that the girls felt this way. But at the end of his tirade he repeated: "All I want is to have her back."

I sat quietly. Sometimes clients come for a session and they need to talk more than they need me to predict something for them. Dennis was a man desperate to get his feelings off his chest. I was the focus for that. He had decided to see me. I knew that the only way I could help him was to try to teach him how to control his thinking. He believed he knew what he wanted. He wanted Kim back. But he had not held on to this desire long enough to give it the necessary energy to make it happen.

He needed to isolate the thought. Dennis's thought of Kim being home was dissipated by the magnitude of the conflicting thoughts and feelings he had about her. He needed to stop complaining and criticizing Kim. Instead, he would have to start directing his thoughts toward the

123

picture of Kim back at home with him. His decision wasn't strong enough to produce a result. He thought his decision to have Kim back home was clear, firm, and unshakable. Yet, he didn't focus on that picture.

Dennis's emotions were causing his picture to become cloudy. If he really wanted Kim home, he had to stop all his resentments and criticism and only focus on the picture of Kim being back home. I explained all of this to Dennis and he listened. I pointed out his conflict and I felt he understood. Dennis decided to use his thought effectively. He focused on seeing Kim home and stopped his negative thoughts about her. His focus on the picture of his wife home with no negative feelings made him happy. This feeling of happiness created positive thought forms, which were received by Kim. She started feeling that she missed him and in time they were able to resolve their problems.

Once you decide what you want, you must take that decision and isolate it from all other thoughts that you have. You must focus your mind on that decision. Isolating and holding the thought is necessary in order to be able to energize it. A thought needs energy to manifest.

When you hold a thought, it produces a picture. For example, if you think "tree," you produce an image of a tree. You don't produce the image of an automobile. In order to get something you must first produce an image of it. This takes focus. The more often you focus on the picture of what you want the faster you will see results. You must see the picture as often as you can. You can train your mind to focus on your picture. This isn't easy and it will take effort on your part but it works.

Rule 2:
SEE IT DONE

Focus your mind on the completed goal, not on the individual steps leading you toward it. Take a direct route to your desire. For example, if you want to go somewhere, you look at a map, find the destination, and then decide which route will get you there most easily. You look at the destination before you leave on your trip. You know where you are going before you know how to get there. You see it done.

The same principle applies when thinking about your goal. If you see yourself having what you want, you will be surprised at how much easier it is to get it.

If you want to go to Italy, see yourself having your passport stamped at the border crossing into Italy. If you want to be married, see yourself at your wedding. If you want to get a master's degree, see yourself at the graduation. If you want to climb Mount Everest, see yourself on the summit. In short, you should always see the end before you see the ways how to get there.

For example, suppose you have to give a speech and you are nervous. Public speaking is not your strength. Picture the room where you deliver your speech. See yourself walking into the room. Now add details. As you look at the audience, see that they are pleased to be there. The aura of the room feels great to you. See the color of the outfit that you are wearing. Watch yourself smile at the audience as you deliver your words. Realize that your speech is terrific. You said everything that you wanted to say and the audience loved it. Hear the applause at the end of your speech. Take a bow and walk out of the room. The more detailed you can make the picture in your mind, the more real it becomes to you. When it becomes more real to you, your belief is intensified. This energizes your resolve and leads you to accomplish your objective.

When you see something done, your mind has projected a powerful image into the atmosphere. This image assures you that you can achieve it. This assurance sends out a potent energy that affects the pace in which this becomes a reality in your life. The more you continue to visualize the same image the clearer it becomes. It becomes more and more real. This intense focus on your completed goal combined with a passionate desire to have it produces a different type of mental energy. This is unlike the energy we use in our everyday thinking.

Our everyday thinking uses physical and emotional energy. For example, when we walk or ride a bike, we use physical energy. When we feel something such as fear or joy, it takes emotional energy. When we *see it done,* we utilize spiritual energy. This energy becomes available when we focus our thought with extreme clarity and intensity.

This energy is available to anyone who has the will and determination to learn how to use it. You have to want to learn to use your thought in a new and powerful manner. You have to practice *seeing it done* just as you would practice playing tennis or golf. The more you practice, the better you will become. You have to focus, concentrate, and envision. The longer you can hold an exact picture in your mind the faster it will be brought into your world.

The quality of thought, the length it is held, and its clarity and intensity determine the manner and the time it takes to materialize. It takes a different energy to launch a rocket than it takes to walk from your kitchen to the front door. It takes more power and force to get the rocket into space. Thoughts have to be launched in order to materialize. They have to be sent out beyond the normal boundaries of the physical world. Many of our thoughts lack energy and force. These thoughts are not able to move into an area of space that will lift them beyond the physical limitations. This level of thought sadly results in failed dreams and goals. When we are able to create thought forms capable of living on a level beyond the norm, we can realize our goals with remarkable ease.

When you have seen something done, you have started a spiritual energy working for you. Get rid of messy thinking. You can't let your thoughts go wild and expect to attract something clear and defined into your life. Common sense helps a great deal. Think in a practical way. Some things are easier to get than others. Some things may take longer, and others can be accomplished quickly. The main objective is to continue the practice of *seeing it done* until you have your goal realized. One thing at a time is the motto. You want to keep your energy focused in the most efficient manner in order to bring whatever you want into your physical world.

It takes time and practice in order to learn how to *see it done.* It takes focus, concentration, and creative visualization. We must train our minds to think differently. Once we have learned how to isolate a thought of what we want and hold this thought, we will learn to picture it in our minds. We will then do this until we are able to bring it into our lives. If you desire to own a restaurant, you must first find time to think of the restaurant and only that. You must concentrate on that restaurant. The next step is to see in your mind's eye a clear picture of yourself having the restaurant. In order to accomplish this, you must be focused, concentrated, and you must learn how to visualize.

Creative Visualization Exercise

We visualize all the time. We think about what we will have for dinner and we create a picture in our mind. Decorators visualize the way a house will look when it's finished. We visualize when we read. How often do we think about the person we are in love with? Everybody visualizes, but we have to learn to visualize in a deeper way. This is a technique. We must learn how to make the images we create in our mind become part of our physical world.

You need to spend fifteen minutes on this exercise. It is very important that you are not interrupted. Find a quiet place. Sit in a comfortable chair with your spine straight and your feet flat on the floor. Close your eyes and let your shoulders drop. Unclench your hands. Let them lie comfortably in your lap or by your sides. Breathe deeply. As you exhale see all the tension leaving your body. Take seven deep inhales and exhales. Seven is the number of creation. Keep your mind focused on your breathing. Thoughts will come into your mind. Don't dwell on them. Bring your mind back to the breath. You should start feeling relaxed. If you don't, take another seven deep inhales and exhales.

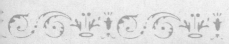

Even if you are still a little tense, go on to the next step of this exercise. Don't despair. You can do the visualization even if you are not completely relaxed. Just do the best you can to be as relaxed as possible.

Now that you have relaxed and your eyes are closed, you are ready to begin your creative visualization. Since it is hard to slow down your mind and focus on one thing or idea, you need a device such as screen. This can be a movie, television, or computer screen. Focus on a blank screen in front of you. Remember, you may want many things. You must choose the thing you want the most.

See a blank screen in your mind's eye. Look at the screen. Begin to create on the screen a picture of having what you want. For example, if you want a house, see yourself holding the key to the property. See yourself walking into your house. See yourself paying the mortgage. Picture yourself happy and content that you finally have the house that you wanted. You may picture the exact physical house if you want to, but create a picture that works for you. As you hold the picture it should become clearer and clearer. You may add details to your picture such as rose bushes in front of your house or a fence surrounding it or shutters on the windows. Details make the picture clearer. The clearer the picture, the more real it becomes in your mind. The most important thing is that you keep your focus on seeing yourself having the house. It is your house. Enjoy this exercise.

It may take some time before you are able to control the flow of your thoughts. Be patient. Whenever an unwanted thought enters onto the screen of your mind let it go and refocus your thought on the picture of the desired object. Bring your mind back to your house. Remember, you are seeing a picture of having what you want. It is done in your mind. After you have held the picture as long as you can, let go of it. You should repeat this exercise often. It takes determination and discipline to find the time. There is no way to train your thoughts to get exactly what you want unless you do this exercise over and over.

It is important that you do anything you can to help bring this about. Don't wait, act. Put yourself out in the world so that you can attract the ways to get the house. You may find that you meet someone who knows of a house at the right price. You may find extra work that brings in additional income. You may fall in love with someone and get a house together. Keep open to all possibilities. Keep your mind flexible.

Debra

Debra could not stay on a diet. When she arrived to see me, her aura showed that she was distraught and greatly disappointed in herself. Her mind was focused on thinking she was fat. Although she had other problems, this was on the forefront of her mind. She had made a firm resolution again on New Year's Eve that she would have the body she always dreamed of. Her resolve lasted less than one week. She not only did not lose weight, but reacting to the depravation of her diet, she binged on every conceivable fattening food. She felt completely hopeless. She arrived at her wits' end. This was the tenth year in a row that she had not been able to keep her resolve.

In the past, Debra had tried low fat, low carb, calorie counting, liquid diet, acupuncture, hypnosis, and fasting in her quest to become thin. I told Debra that the problem was not what she ate but what she thought. She had to change her approach in order to achieve her goal. She asked me what to do. The first thing she needed to do was to *see it done.* She needed to create a clear, precise image of herself looking thin and healthy. She must hold this image and bring it into her mind as many times a day as possible. She should hold this for at least two minutes at a time. She could add details to her picture. Perhaps she could see herself on the beach in a bathing suit, on a date with a fabulous guy, or shopping for the most fashionable clothes. She must not let the picture lose strength. No matter what happens, even if she breaks down and eats the wrong food, she must still take time to focus on *seeing it done,* seeing herself with the body that she desires. The longer and the more often she is able to concentrate on the visual image of herself thin, the more powerful her resolve will become.

"Debra, do you believe you deserve to look the way you want to?" I asked.

"What do you mean?" she replied with real confusion.

"Debra, tell me about your mother. I perceive that when you were young, she criticized your looks. She told you that you would never be thin. You began to believe this was true. This belief created a false concept in your mind. Of course you can be thin. You must replace the false concept that keeps playing over and over in your mind with a true one. You must replace the negative image that you have pictured in your mind. You have the power to do this. Once you change the picture your resolution will succeed."

Debra started to cry and then sobbed. I had hit the nail on the head. Debra had never been able to get over the words of her mother. She believed she would fail, so she failed. This was the root cause of her inability to keep her New Year's resolution.

"Debra," I said, "you can't change the past, but you can shape the future. If you know what you want and *see it done,* you are halfway there. Your mind creates the picture and persistence increases the power of the image. The image will propel you toward it. The ideal method for achieving your desire will come to you. It may be immediate or it may take a short while, but if you don't give up, the way will be shown. Do not allow yourself to go negative, Debra. If you feel yourself weakening, flash the picture of how you want to look, and this will help you."

A year passed and Debra came back to see me. She looked terrific. The realization that she was allowing her mother's negative words to rule her life was like a wake-up call. The same day she left our last session, she started visualizing herself thin. Her resolve did not falter this time. Even when she broke down and had the cookies or the cake, she forced her mind to refocus on the picture. This mental exercise kept her from dropping the diet idea altogether. Debra knew that walking was a good way to lose weight. One late afternoon she decided to walk home from work. On her way she ran into a girl she had not seen for two years. This girl had lost sixty pounds. Debra asked her how she did this. She told her it was Weight Watchers. Debra joined Weight Watchers. She continued to visualize herself thin. This, combined with the diet and the walking, resulted in making her New Year's resolution a reality.

New Year's resolutions are a good idea because they can give the mind focus. They can strengthen the will. Any decision made with firm belief produces a powerful picture in the mind. But why do so many people break their resolutions? They start out positive that they will keep their resolve. In a short time their determination falters. When you train your mind to see it done first, you will succeed. Even if you have failed in the past, keep making resolutions. The action of turning your thought toward a positive change in your life has a profound effect. If you don't succeed, try and try again. *See it done.*

Lou

Lou called me for advice because he could not find a job. He was worried and depressed. I told him he needed to see himself working. He should picture himself in his mind's eye leaving the house on his way to a job. He should see himself putting his paycheck in the bank. See this picture as often as possible and proceed to look actively for employment. I explained that by seeing the job done, he would attract the position with greater ease.

Lou took my advice. He saw a picture of himself happily working, making enough to eliminate financial worry. He ran this picture like a movie on the screen over and over. He called me a few weeks later. He'd run into an old friend from college who knew of a job and Lou got it. Lou was amazed by the swift change of circumstances. "This isn't magic," I told Lou. "This is the result of your right thinking."

Rule 3: DON'T VACILLATE

Vacillate means to waver, to change your mind, to not commit. We vacillate because we are unsure. This

results in fluctuating thoughts. A fear of failure and disappointment comes into our minds. Release those thoughts. Remain steadfast. Otherwise, you do not hold on to a single specific thought long enough to bring it into our world. Like a pendulum swinging in the air if our minds go back and forth, we go nowhere. If you try to glue a handle back on a cup, you have to hold the handle long enough so the glue can set. If you don't, the handle will fall off again.

Let's say you want true love. You are lonely and believe it is time that you meet the love of your life. Instead of spending time focusing on love and concentrating on seeing yourself happy in love, your mind rambles: "I'll never find it," "Nothing ever works out for me," "I am too old," "I don't know where to meet anyone" or "I am great," "Someone is lucky to have me," "I will take a trip to Club Med," "No, I will go to the bars with my girlfriend," "No, I will call a dating service," "No, I will go to Central Park and see who is playing soccer," and on and on. You go over in your mind all the loves that have turned out badly. Then you reminisce about your wonderful love from high school. All these thoughts will get you nowhere. You must stop them. The only way to stop chaotic thinking is to focus.

Worry can cause us to vacillate. If you are in the middle of a marathon and one minute you are thinking, "I can finish the marathon," and then the next minute you are thinking, "It's impossible, I am exhausted, I can't do it," you will have trouble finishing the race.

When you vacillate, you weaken your resolve and lose willpower. Nothing can be accomplished without a strong will. A thought becomes weak when the mind hesitates and starts wavering. Doubt sets in. This is dangerous because it can bring forth the opposite of your original goal. The dominant picture that you hold in your mind will come into being. The strong always prevails over the weak. Vacillating means you're questioning your decision.

When you vacillate, you either don't know what you want, are uncertain about your ability to get it, or don't believe you deserve to have it. Winners don't vacillate, losers do. Success is achieved by those who are decisive. Decisive people don't doubt themselves. They are crystal clear about what they want and their ability to get it.

Typical thoughts from the minds of vacillators are:

> *"Yes, I can do it—no, I can't."*
> *"I am good enough—no, I am not."*

139

"Yes, I can handle it—no, it's too hard."

"I want this—I am not sure."

"I believe this will work—but maybe it won't."

"Should I do it—should I not do it?"

"He loves me—no, I am being silly."

Carol

The first thing I saw when Carol walked into my office was that her aura emanated a shade of yellow that indicated her great talent and intellect. Carol wanted to write a book. She felt strongly about this. She made an appointment to see me hoping that I could see a bestseller in her future. But Carol was indecisive. First she wanted to write a novel, but no, "novels are too long." She would write nonfiction, but she didn't know what subject to write about. Then she thought maybe she ought to write a children's book. She realized that she didn't understand children. Then she decided to write a book of short stories. However, on further thought, she realized that she didn't even like to read short stories so why would she write one.

Carol's strong inability to decide what to write was making me dizzy. I did not see a finished book in

Carol's future. I saw the talent and the ability. She had discipline and time but she lacked decisiveness.

"Make up your mind, Carol!" I said. "Once you've made a decision about the type of book you would like to write, it could be done quickly. But if you keep fluctuating, you will never be published. That would be very sad because it's a tragedy to waste talent like yours.

"Focus on seeing a published book with your name on it. You do not have to see the title of the book. Just picture yourself in your mind on your book tour holding your book and being happy. Hold that picture for at least two minutes at a time. You should do this exercise often. When you finish the exercise, let the picture go. It may take some time to decide which book you want to write. But if you persist in your decision to write a book and continue to see it done you will succeed. It's in your hands, Carol; I cannot predict whether or not you will use your discipline to make up your mind. You have no problem except you lack confidence and this negative thinking is causing you to remain indecisive."

Carol must have taken my words to heart because two years later I was standing in a bookstore and under the heading "New Fiction" I saw a book written by her.

You must not succumb to other people's indecisive thoughts or differing opinions. If you are absolutely certain about something, go for it. Don't listen to those who disagree. Don't allow their negative thoughts to get into your aura. Keep a mental shield around yourself so these disharmonious thoughts cannot affect you. This does not imply that you should live in a fantasy, never paying attention to what anyone else says. It means don't fall prey to the voices of doom or allow yourself to vacillate because you listened to people who don't know anything about your decision. These thoughts usually originate from the minds of jealous, insecure, uneducated, or indecisive people.

Thomas

Thomas, a twenty-eight-year-old salesperson, was living at home with his parents. He was desperate to find a home of his own. He decided to buy an apartment. He told his friend Michael about his decision. Michael was not supportive. He told Thomas, "You are crazy. You cannot possibly afford to do that. You don't make enough money."

This made Thomas pause and rethink his decision. Thomas then spoke to another friend. This friend had a great deal of experience dealing in real estate. He told Thomas, "Of course, you can buy an apartment. Talk to someone in real estate." This made Thomas feel better. It helped to strengthen his resolve.

Thomas then remembered his sister had a friend who was a real estate agent. He called, they met, and the agent said, "Based on your salary alone, it will be difficult to make this happen. Do you have a cosigner or do you have someone who could lend you money for a down payment? Let's run some numbers and consider the options."

Together they worked out a possible scenario for a deal. This included the targeted purchase price, size of the apartment, monthly outlay, and down payment. She showed Thomas some apartments that fit the scenario. Thomas knew he was getting closer to finding a way to swing the deal. But he wasn't there yet. How would he come up with the down payment or someone to cosign?

He went home and asked his parents if they could help him. His father wasn't supportive and refused to help. He told Thomas he was too young to afford an apartment. This was a big blow. Thomas became disil-

143

lusioned for a little while. What could he do? He didn't have an answer. But he kept the thought of buying an apartment in his mind. He saw it done.

A few weeks later, he was at a family reunion. His grandmother noticed that Thomas did not seem like himself. "You look worried. What's the matter?" He told her about his desire to buy an apartment. She listened intently and said, "I will help you." He had never expected that. She agreed to cosign. Thomas was elated. He started looking at apartments in his price range. What he saw was disappointing, but he kept looking until he found one he could afford. Everything was in place. Grandmother cosigned for the mortgage. However, at the last minute, he panicked because he realized that the closing costs were higher than he had expected. He could not possibly ask his grandmother for more money. He had doubts whether or not he could come up with the needed cash. At the eleventh hour his uncle Jack, hearing about the apartment drama, offered to give Thomas the rest of the money to close. Thomas got the apartment.

If Thomas had succumbed to Michael's voice of doom or given up because his father didn't help him, he wouldn't have closed the deal. Knowing he looked bad on paper could have stopped him as well. He was able to beat the odds because he ultimately did not vacillate. He had made up his mind and did not let the negative thoughts of others undermine his resolve. He had done his homework and gathered enough information to be secure in his knowledge that he could afford the apartment. It was not easy, and even at the last minute it looked doomed. But he continued to be convinced that he could find a way to close the deal. And he did.

When we create an image in our mind of any particular thing we desire, we either have an image of ourselves having it or we have an image of ourselves not having it.

Clara

Clara wants to get married. She is forty-two years old and has never had a long-term relationship, but she wants to get married. She vacillates between believing she will be married and feeling it won't happen. One image in her mind is married, happy, secure, and in love. The other image she holds is herself as a spinster, unhappy, broke, and lonely.

Clara tries to keep focused on marriage. Then she reads an article in a woman's magazine about singles.

The article gives statistics showing that the odds for getting married after the age of forty are not good. This causes her thoughts of marriage to weaken and she sees the image of herself again alone. Then she is able to set her mind on the image of getting married. This leads her to go to a specific event designed for singles who want to get married. Unfortunately, not one man that she considered attractive wanted to talk with her. As she left the event, the dominant image in her mind was again unmarried, lonely, and old. But Clara did not give up. Again, she focused on marriage and decided to post a listing on a website for people wanting to get married. She did this for six months but could not find anyone who was even a possibility for marriage. This caused her again to hold the image of a spinster.

Clara kept telling her friends about her lack of success in finding a marriage partner. Every time she had a discussion with someone relating her failure to find a mate, she was holding in her mind the image of being unmarried. Clara is still single.

The lesson for all of us is that if we continually see ourselves as lonely, powerless, unhappy, poor, or sick, we make it a great deal easier to manifest these attributes. Like a baker who pours batter into the bread mold, we create a mold for these negatives to manifest into our lives. Conversely, if we think harmony, health, love, good fortune, and happiness these are equally sure to occur.

■ *Rule 4:* YOU MUST HAVE FAITH

Faith is belief. Nothing can be accomplished without it. Many people struggle with faith, but maybe they wouldn't if they took a minute to think about all the things we do that rely on faith. We execute actions through faith all the time without thinking. The act of walking is performed because we have a full and unflinching faith that we can do this. We cross the road when the light is green because we believe the cars will stop. We go to a doctor trusting he can treat our problem. We fill a prescription confident that the pharmacist will give us the right medicine. We sign contracts believing the terms will be met. We hire accountants trusting they will correctly prepare our tax returns. We go to confession believing our sins will be forgiven. There are countless actions we take every day that are based on

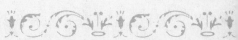

faith. Faith gives us confidence. It gives us focus. It strengthens the will. Faith allows the will to act without tension. Faith leads us to expect results.

When we will something to happen, we direct our thought toward the desired goal. For example, "I will stop smoking," "I will lose weight," "I will get a promotion," "I will find a way." The stronger the will, the more energy we have accumulated. This energy is focused directly on our goal.

When we have faith that we can do something, we find the way to do it. We don't doubt that we will succeed. Faith produces a superior imagination, which helps us to come up with ideas to make things happen. This makes it easier to achieve our goals.

Faith, which is constructive thought, helps things materialize. Faith can be acquired. Positive thinking strengthens faith. Concentration and focus strengthens faith. This type of thought is constructive and guides us toward taking useful action. Useful actions produce a feeling of accomplishment. This feeling builds confidence. Your commitment to be successful is made stronger. Doubt paralyzes us and leads to mistakes and inaction.

Faith strengthens the will and allows us to think on an elevated level. This combination produces what is not yet visible. The will is a power created through concentration. Will power is a major element in bringing our desires into our life. Absolute belief that something will happen focuses the will on the attainment of the goal. Faith gives us a sense of peace, security, and trust. Faith allows the will to act without tension. The will finds ways to make things happen and does not stop until success is complete. True will power is a quality of the spirit. The spirit, the higher part of the mind, is connected with the Divine Force. Nothing can be accomplished without faith. Hope sets up a thought of disbelief and this thought will undermine you. Faith sets up the thought of obtaining and this will benefit you.

I have been asked many times, "How do you acquire faith?" My answer is: "The only way to develop faith is to act." Faith produces powerful productive thought forms. Any action taken with belief is easier to accomplish. The desire to have faith will lead you toward having it. When your mind is in doubt, you must turn your thought toward the Divine Force.

Exercise for Faith

Take a deep breath and ask the Divine Force to help you:

"Divine Force, give me confidence."

"Divine Force, strengthen my will."

Doubt can't have power over you unless you give it power. Write down all of the things you can think of that take faith. Learn from others. Observe the behavior of the faithful and try to emulate their actions.

Darla

Faith gives us courage. Darla, a thirty-year-old woman who lives in Nashville went to the Rocky Mountains on vacation. While there she decided she would like to go hiking. She had little experience, but felt she was in good shape from her regular workouts back home.

Darla bought a guidebook and chose what seemed to be an easy, well-marked trail. Darla was enjoying her hike so much that when she reached the end of her chosen trail she decided to continue on. There was a sign pointing to another trail that would lead her to a higher point, which would afford a much better view.

Her lack of experience made it impossible for her to evaluate just how long it would take her to get to her new destination and back. It also prevented her from realizing how quickly the weather can change. A few clouds developed and the temperature dropped. She was getting colder and colder. It had been warm when she started so she'd left her heavy jacket in her car. She looked up and saw more clouds moving in quickly. Moments later she was amazed to see that it had started snowing.

She realized that she had to get down the mountain as fast as she could. It would soon be too dark to see.

151

The snow got heavier and her clothes were getting wet. Her lack of experience did not serve her well. She had no idea that it could even snow this early in the year. She was not prepared. Time was not on her side. Having only planned to hike for a few hours, she did not have adequate food or water. She was hungry and thirsty. The wet snow chilled her to the bone. She began to feel tired and confused. She was getting so wet that she thought maybe she should try to find some sort of shelter. But then she thought it would be better to get down the mountain.

In her fatigue, she missed a turn and went off the trail. It took her about an hour before she started having doubts whether or not she was walking in the right direction. The weather was getting worse. She started to become afraid. She decided she'd better look for shelter, rest a little, and wait until the snow stopped to make it easier to find the way down the mountain. But there was no obvious shelter.

She decided to sit under a tree. The snowfall became heavier. Fear enveloped her. She had never felt so alone. She knew there was nothing to do but to pray for help. This act of praying calmed Darla. She replaced the fear with resolve to find a way to get out of this situation. At that point, it had become really dark and even colder. Darla did not lose the faith that she would be all right. She got up from under the tree. She started jumping up and down in order to get the blood flowing through her body. This made her feel a little warmer.

Darla decided to start singing at the top of her voice. She was afraid of animals. The singing kept her mind occupied on something that was positive. She sang every song she could think of. When she became too cold, she stopped singing and started to jump up and down again. She did not know how long this went on. She was not aware that hours had passed. As she kept her faith other ideas came to her mind. She knew enough to stay put and close to the tree for shelter. When she became too tired, she would think about the things she would do as soon as she was down the mountain.

In the meantime, the owner of the small bed-and-breakfast where she was staying became concerned when he did not see her in the evening. She had left a message with him saying that she was going hiking. About six o'clock he began to wonder where Darla was. Then he thought maybe she went out for dinner after her hike and thought she would be back later. When it got to be eleven and he had not seen her, he became worried. He knew a ranger of the search and rescue team and called to tell him about Darla. The ranger said, "Let's wait another hour and see if she shows up. If not, we better start looking for her. Do you know where she went?"

The hotel owner was not sure but he had suggested to Darla a trail that she might have liked because he felt the hike was scenic and not too difficult. After one hour when she had not returned the ranger started out with two others to try to find Darla.

After they had been searching that part of the mountain for a few hours one of the rangers of the rescue team heard singing. He called the other rangers. They could not believe it at first but there it was. It took them a while to pinpoint where exactly the voice was coming from. Then they started moving toward the voice, yelling and calling her name. When they reached Darla, she was in remarkable spirits under the circumstances. They immediately gave her a warm blanket, water, and food. One of the rescuers said to her: "How in the world did you handle this?"

"I prayed for help and here you are. I never for one minute lost my faith that I would make it back down the mountain."

Darla kept her faith even though she was cold, confused, and disoriented. Even when her plight seemed worse and fear set in she kept the faith. This gave her ideas for surviving. Darla proves that faith strengthens the will and elevates the imagination.

Owen

Owen owns a lumber company in Ohio. A few years ago he ran into big trouble. A fire in the lumber yard destroyed his inventory. He tried to collect insurance but the insurance company would not pay the claim. The insurance adjuster said that Owen did not have the proper documentation proving his inventory. As a result, the insurance company refused to pay.

Owen was shocked and distraught. He was positive that he had complied with the terms of the insurance policy. He had paid a very high premium to ensure that his inventory was fully covered. Owen had no alternative but to hire an attorney and to fight the insurance company. The attorney felt that Owen had an excellent case but that it might take time until he could recover what was owed him. The attorney reviewed the case but told Owen, "I will take the case, but we will probably have to sue them. That always takes time and money."

Owen did not have time or money. The loss of his inventory made it impossible to fulfill his orders. Since

he could not meet his orders, he had no cash flow. Having won a large construction job right before the fire, he had put his own money into increasing his inventory. He had exhausted his bank accounts to meet several payrolls. He was trying to keep his regular, full-time staff employed, knowing there were no jobs for them in this small town. Having no cash flow he could not pay his bills.

The first thing he tried to do was get a loan from the local bank. Although they wanted to help him, he did not have any collateral. He then offered his house as collateral, but there was very little equity available. This would not solve his problems. When that did not work, he turned to his suppliers. He tried to negotiate an agreement with his suppliers. He asked them to extend to him sufficient long-term credit for the purchase of supplies. But they would not give it to him because they felt he was too close to going under.

Owen would not give up. He felt in his heart that he could pull through this crisis. His brother felt terrible because he could not help. He thought about his assets. What could he sell to bring in cash? He had machinery for moving logs and saws to cut lumber among other equipment.

Owen put the word out that he was selling. No

offers came in. Things were getting worse by the minute. He could no longer meet payroll. But Owen kept up the fight. He believed there must be a way. His bookkeeper, Mayme, had been with him for thirty years. She knew the extent of the problems. Mayme went to Owen and told him she would remain on the job. He could pay her as soon as the business had turned around. This generosity deeply moved Owen. Mayme's example inspired the others. Three more of the employees offered to work with their pay deferred, which helped, but the problems remained. Owen needed money now.

The attorney's reports were not bad, but it became clear that there would be no quick resolution. They would be lucky if they could win the case within a year.

Owen was indeed worried, but somehow he knew deep inside that everything would be all right. He would get the money and save the business. Other businessmen in town talked among themselves. They all thought that Owen would have to close the business. He was well liked and known as a kind man honorable in business. But no one had the funds to bail him out.

As a last resort, he considered trying to find a partner and sell half his business. He remembered that there was a broker in a larger town about an hour's drive away. He made an appointment to see him. The broker told Owen that he might be able to help him, but a deal like this takes on average eight to twelve months. Owen left the meeting realizing this option would not save him. He didn't have that kind of time.

Yet, he still had faith and continued to focus his mind on coming up with a solution. About a week after the meeting with the broker, Mayme invited Owen to a picnic at her home in celebration of her fortieth wedding anniversary. Owen felt rather low and didn't want to go to a picnic. But he could not disappoint Mayme on such a special occasion. He forced himself to go. Owen, always a gentleman, did his best to be social. After an hour he began to think it was okay to leave. He had talked to most of the guests. Then he heard someone yell his name. He turned around and saw a man whom he did not immediately recognize. The man came closer and said, "Don't you remember me? I beat you every time at wrestling in high school."

"Oh, my word, Norm Hansen. I haven't seen you in thirty-five years. What are you doing here?"

"I am related to the groom. You better sit down and have a beer with me. You can't leave. I just got here."

Owen sat down, happy to see this old friend. Ultimately, he told Norm that he had been having some

troubles with his lumber company. Norm pressed him for the details. Owen reluctantly filled him in. Before the picnic was over, Norm offered Owen a loan in an amount that saved the business. As it turned out, Norm had just sold a very lucrative business. A year later, the insurance lawsuit was won. Owen repaid Norm. The company survived.

We most often acquire faith through experience. The importance of faith cannot be stressed enough. The act of desiring faith will lead you to experiences that will give you the faith you seek. Faith produces an elevated state of the imagination. This superior type of imagination allows us to see things that are not yet visible to the physical eye. It strengthens the will and keeps doubts away. Faith gives us focus. Faith gives us trust, security, and an open mind. We believe we will be guided toward that which is best for us and we will be.

■ *Rule 5:*
PERSISTENCE REAPS RESULTS

Persistence builds strength around your thoughts. It is the ability to keep pursuing your goals despite adversities. It means not giving up no matter what possible impediments must be overcome. For example, you cannot focus, concentrate, or visualize. Maybe you get discouraged because you cannot see results, lose faith, feel it is too hard, or want to give up.

How many times have you started something and not finished it? At the beginning you were excited, energetic, determined, and upbeat. It could have been learning a foreign language, dancing the tango, playing the piano, or any other pursuit. Then, in time, interest waned and you quit. Later on did you say to yourself, you wished you had persisted?

Persistence is required to become proficient in anything, be it a carpenter, electrician, court reporter, athlete, artist, or musician. In order to use the power of thought you must visualize your objective over and over again until it is realized. Thought becomes alive through clarity, intensity, and repetition. The persistence of the thinker gives the thought energy. This energy, when clearly directed, reaps results.

Janet

You may not be aware that it is easier to walk on water than to obtain a lease for a rent-stabilized apartment in New York City. Everyone will tell you that you are living in a fantasy if you say that you are looking for one. My client, Janet, proved that sometimes, if you don't give up, fantasies become realities.

Janet came to New York from Ohio to be an actress. Her dream was to be on Broadway and live in Greenwich Village. She had grown up seeing movies about New York City. Her favorite—*Funny Face*—took place in New York's Greenwich Village. The movie, starring Audrey Hepburn, had made an indelible impression on her. Greenwich Village seemed exciting, romantic, artsy, fun; in short, where everything was happening.

Janet came to New York and received a rude awakening. There were almost no apartments available in Greenwich Village and those that were came with exorbitant prices. She put her dream on hold and took a studio apartment in Flushing, Queens.

Like many struggling actresses Janet got a job as a waitress. Flexible hours made it possible to attend classes and go to auditions. She never for one moment gave up her belief that she would be successful in her

career and get an apartment in Greenwich Village. She asked everyone she met if they knew of any rent-stabilized apartments available. They often just laughed at her and gave no encouragement at all.

Every morning Janet checked the newspapers, the online listings, and postings on bulletin boards. This went on for two years. There were times when Janet felt weary, but it never occurred to her to give up. One day Janet decided to try a dance class she had heard good things about. She was not a dancer but enjoyed it for the exercise. At the end of class she noticed a girl rubbing her ankle as if she was in pain. Janet introduced herself and asked the girl if she needed help. Her name was Marci and she appeared to be in low spirits. Janet said, "Let's go to Starbucks, and I will buy you a cup of coffee."

Marci talked about her frustration. She had been auditioning for months and had not gotten a job yet. Her ankle was causing her a great deal of pain, making everything seem more difficult. Janet told Marci about a Chinese practitioner known for his expertise with this type of injury. After an hour Marci realized she didn't know anything about Janet. She asked Janet the typical questions New Yorkers ask: "What do you do, where do you live?" Janet of course told her about her need to find a rent-stabilized apartment in Greenwich Village. Marci said, "I know someone who has a rent-stabilized apartment that she doesn't need anymore. Do you want to see it?" Janet was too stunned to speak for a moment. "Of course, I do, but why don't you want it?" "Oh, my husband and I own an apartment on the Upper West Side. We're all set. My aunt has had this apartment for thirty years. She is finally getting married and is moving to his house in Connecticut. She doesn't like the city anymore, is rarely in the apartment, and is ready to give it up."

Janet got the apartment. It was in one of those rare buildings where new tenants could rent vacated apartments under stabilization guidelines. Initially, the rent increase was twenty percent and after that it was raised according to the guidelines. Janet was ecstatic. Her friends did not believe it until they saw the apartment. Persistence had won.

Every year you hear about many small businesses that fail. Many times there were outside circumstances beyond their control that caused the business to close. But on examination, it is evident that lack of persis-

tence by the owners was the root of the demise. People gave up when they could have continued.

Vincent

When Vincent came to see me, he was successful in New York real estate. Faced with bankruptcy because of a recession, he fought and saved his business. Many others in the same business went under. I asked Vincent, "How did you survive?" He told me the banks were no longer lending money. Some of his tenants had moved; others stayed but were unable to pay the rents. Nothing was selling. It was impossible to pay his expenses. But he refused to sell the properties at a huge loss. He believed that real estate always came back if you hold on to it. He never faltered in his belief that he could find a way to survive.

He borrowed as much as he could from relatives. This kept him afloat and bought him some time. But it was still nip and tuck. He was teetering on the verge of folding. But he kept his mind focused on finding a solution. He closed his Fifth Avenue office and set up his business at his home. This saved a great deal of money.

Then it occurred to him that he was not alone in his struggle to survive the recession. Many businesses

were desperate to get money. After some soul-searching he came up with an idea. Why not become a mortgage broker for people like himself, who owned commercial rental properties? He would need a license. He took an accelerated course, which required him to study night and day. He was exhausted at the end of it but he passed the test. He joined a known mortgage brokerage firm, negotiating an agreement where he would receive a draw against future commissions. This draw was enough to keep him afloat.

He put the word out that he was now in the mortgage brokerage business and relentlessly pursued all his contacts. It did not take long until he was able to line up a number of prospective clients. He knew that the New York banks would be hesitant to lend money to his clients, so he put his mind to finding funding from banks in other states. In one case, after a great deal of searching and a lot of effort, he found a bank in Arizona that would lend the money. Once he had closed his first deal, the next came easier.

This was the beginning of a lucrative second career for Vincent. When the recession ended, Vincent did not need to be a mortgage broker any longer. He went back full force into his original business: real estate. Despite opening up a new business, he never took his eye off his original decision to save his business. His determination successfully carried him through the difficulties.

It takes persistence to learn how to use the rules in order to get what you want. You have to learn to focus, to visualize, and not to vacillate. You have to keep the faith, stay positive, and not give up. With persistence you will learn how to control your thoughts and your life will change.

This may seem too easy. The simplicity may make you doubt, but simplicity itself takes effort at first. Doubt freezes the will and makes a person ineffective. It takes a firm commitment to change your thinking and to learn to discipline your thoughts. You will feel like you are training different muscles in your brain and you are. You are allowing the mind, the higher part of the brain, to do the thinking. This type of thought vibrates faster than our normal thinking because it is composed of less gross matter. It is less material and solid but more magnetic and etheric. Speed and magnetism are a potent combination for bringing objects into form. It is amazing when you start to see the results of your thoughts.

I know this from personal experience. I have written four books. I have always seen a clear picture of the completed book before I began writing. In short, I have seen the books done. This has helped me to focus on developing the ideas for each book. I would also see clear pictures of myself at the bookstores signing copies for my readers.

Everything in your life will be affected by your new mode of thinking. Thinking is being raised to an art form. To perfect any art it takes focus, determination, vision, and persistence. Keep your mind flexible, open to new things. You will be amazed at what will be presented to you.

Gratitude inspires faith

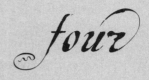

TOOLS TO
HELP IMPLEMENT
THE RULES

I t takes discipline to learn anything new. In time, with practice, the rules become easier to follow and eventually they become integrated into your life. With integration there is no longer a need for discipline. You'll find you enjoy using what you have learned. Tools can help us in this process. They can be a valuable support.

Tools can help us implement the rules. These tools that I give you are very powerful. I know because I use them. These tools will help you to isolate a thought, focus on it, and concentrate on a deeper level for a longer period of time. They will also help you to keep from vacillating and make visualizations easier. You do not have to use all of the tools. You may wish to use only some of the tools. They are there to provide support if needed.

■ MOZART'S MUSIC

Mozart makes people happy. In 2006, I visited Vienna, Austria, during the celebrations of Wolfgang Amadeus Mozart's two hundred fiftieth birthday. The celebrations lasted the entire year. Some three hundred thousand people visited the newly renovated Mozart house. This house, where Mozart lived the longest, vibrated with such extraordinary energy that I would not have been surprised to see him walk through the door. Vienna was alive with Mozart. One of the most beautiful monuments that I have ever seen sits in the garden of the Hapsburg winter palace. It is a glorious statue of a young, vibrant Mozart. The statue is set on a platform. There is a beautiful green lawn in front of the monument. There are chairs on both sides of flower beds, which have been magnificently molded into a large G clef. I sat on one of the chairs and observed the continuous flow of people coming to see the statue and have their picture taken. There were people from all walks of life and from all parts of the world. Everyone was happy and smiling, hugging one another. People could not get close enough. They wanted to put their cheeks against the statue. They wanted to put their arms around the statue. It was obvious that everybody loved Mozart. Mozart makes people happy. Mozart's thoughts live through his music.

Music is thinking with melody. Music has vibration, color, and form. People who are psychically gifted can see a color when they hear the striking of a chord of music. Music is manifestation of emotion. Music speaks to the soul. It creates moods. It has healing power. Pythagoras found that music could heal mental illnesses by producing certain chords on a lyre, a seven-stringed instrument. Today some health practitioners are beginning to use music in operating rooms and physical therapy sessions.

There is a form of inspiration where the person's mind is elevated to such a spiritual level that this person becomes a direct channel for the Divine Force. The greatest of all inspiration comes directly from the Divine Force. Mozart is an example of this channel.

During my stay in Vienna I experienced this firsthand. There is a concert hall called the Sala Terrena. It is the oldest concert hall in Vienna, where Mozart used to work and play for Archbishop Colloredo in 1781.

A house is connected to this concert hall that Mozart lived in from March 16 to May 2, 1781. The Sala Terrena is beautiful. Its walls and ceiling are covered with floral paintings and sensual scenes. I was reminded of buildings I had seen in Venice. The acoustics are superb and the atmosphere is wonderful. The four chamber musicians were dressed as they would have been in Mozart's time. The musicians began by playing Divertimento D-Dur K. 136, followed by Eine Kleine Nachtmusik K. 525 and Dissonanzen-Quartet K. 465. From the moment the first chord was struck until the last note of the concert was played I psychically saw an intense white light filling the room and seemingly coming from beyond the ceiling. The power radiating from these notes produced octaves of pure violet with golden stars. As the music continued, I saw all the colors of the rainbow. I have seen auras since I was a small child. I have seen forms coming from musical notes, but I have never experienced such divine hues of color combined with startling, dramatic forms enveloped in iridescent white light. I had always loved Mozart's music and felt spiritual vibrations from it. But this experience gave me a much deeper insight into Mozart. His music possesses an unearthly power. That is why it is known to affect people's thinking, health, and creativity. I had a mystical experience as I listened and psychically saw the Divine Force pouring from his notes. This room had an added impact because Mozart himself had played here. This is how I knew that Mozart was a channel for the Divine Force.

The Divine Force was working through Mozart at all times. Mozart had all his compositions finished in his head. He would often frustrate and frighten the musicians who were going to play one of his symphonies. There were times when he did not hand them the sheet music until twenty minutes before a performance was to begin. Sometimes the ink was still wet as the musicians had their first glance at what they were to perform. Mozart had absolute faith that he would get the music written on paper in time for the musician's performances. And he did.

People would be astonished that Mozart liked to write while there was a lot of activity going on around him. He hated to be alone. He could be writing one of his operas and be involved in a game of billiards at the same time. He would drop his pen and manuscript paper and take his turn shooting at billiards. He would go right back and continue writing down a great aria. The Divine Force flowed so powerfully through Mozart that he was able to compose anywhere, anytime, and anyplace. He did not need controlled circumstances.

On more than one occasion, after he completed a performance of his music on the pianoforte, he was asked by someone if they could see the sheet music. Mozart would sheepishly hand them a blank paper, because he had performed the music completely from memory. He had never written it down. If asked, he could reproduce the piece again exactly as he had played it. The music came completely from his mind. When Mozart would be asked how he did that, where that composition came from, he would often say, "I do not know where it comes from, it is just there. It's in my head."

When people are sick, you are always told: Be quiet. When you are studying or trying to concentrate you will often say, "Cut the noise, I can't hear myself think." These things are never said when Mozart's music is playing. Mozart's music stimulates concentration. It sets a mood that makes you contemplative. Some of the pieces are magnificent background music for meditation. Listen to Mozart and choose pieces that make you feel centered.

Mozart's music has psychic power. This music has inspired, calmed, and healed many people. It has a hypnotic effect. Psychically, I can see the magnificent colors and thought forms that flow from this music. Therefore, I suggest if you have trouble with any of the rules, be it isolating a thought, deciding what you want, seeing it done, staying focused (not to vacillate), keeping faith, or remaining persistent, listen to Mozart. His music is magical.

There are over six hundred Mozart pieces to choose from. It could be overwhelming trying to decide which piece is the most useful for your specific problem and following the rules of thinking. Any Mozart music that you like will work. Buy a CD. Try listening to Mozart in your car, at home, or in you office. Play Mozart to your children. Let them grow up with Mozart. This will help them to be calm, to study, to concentrate, to grow up in greater harmony. They will have better grades in school. They will also get along better with other children.

The following Mozart pieces are ones that I have found to be particularly helpful to me. I selected my favorites pieces for each rule. Over the years, I have shared these suggestions with many clients and friends.

Rule 1: You Must Decide What You Want

Piano Concerto No. 23, K. 488, Adagio,

approximately six minutes

It has a sublime sound that leads to deep contemplation. I find that it lends itself to focusing and deciding what you want. You will also find that this particular piece is very powerful for meditating on the Divine Force.

Rule 2: See It Done

Concerto for Flute and Harp, K. 299,

approximately nine minutes

The music is elegant, with flawless balance between the flute and the harp. The composition gives the mind clarity.

Rule 3: Don't Vacillate

Piano Concerto No. 21, K. 467, Andante,

approximately seven minutes

The combination of notes has a focusing effect and helps you not to waver; the music starts romantic, but becomes mystical. It lends itself to meditating on the Divine Force and helps with problem solving.

Rule 4: You Must Have Faith
Violin Concerto No. 3 in G, K. 216,
eight-and-a-half minutes
This piece is clear, direct, and smooth. The violin seems to lead the listener into a visionary world. The violin and flute appear to be conversing with each other. This selection is also suitable for strengthening your faith.

Rule 5: Persistence Reaps Results
Adagio for Violin and Orchestra, K. 261, *a little over 7 minutes*
You feel as if the violin leads you on a path forward, an optimistic road. The music will help when things are difficult.

Meditation

Flute Quartet No. 1, K. 285, Adagio, *almost three minutes*
The music is mystical; it takes thought to another level; puts you into the mood for meditation through its other-worldly sound.

Andante, K. 315, *six-and-a-half minutes*
The music is soothing, yet the flute leads the listener like the Pied Piper. It makes you feel strong and positive.

Music is thinking
with melody

■ BREATHING FOR RELAXATION AND FOCUS

Breathing helps us relax. When we are relaxed we focus better and our concentration improves. This exercise will relax you and help prepare you to focus and concentrate. This exercise will also help if you find yourself in a situation that makes you feel anxious or negative.

Sit with your spine straight on a chair. Put your feet flat on the floor. Close your eyes and inhale on three counts. Hold your breath for three counts. Exhale on the count of three. Relax. Just concentrate on the breath and nothing else. If your mind wanders, bring it back to the counting of the breath. Do this five times.

For those who are ready for a bigger challenge: Stand with your feet apart. Slowly raise your arms above your head while you inhale on a count of seven. Exhale on a count of seven. Then inhale while you hold your arms above your head on the count of seven. Exhale while you lower your arms back to your sides on a count of seven. Repeat this exercise.

■ CANDLE

A candle is a great tool to help us focus because fire is connected to spirit. When we think on a spiritual level, we think at a faster rate of vibration. This rate of vibration has an effect on the energy that our thought is comprised of. In order to bring anything into form we must focus. The more intense we are able to focus the more quickly we will be successful.

Single Candle

Place a candle on an uncluttered surface at a distance that is comfortable to you. Light the candle. Now focus on the flame and only the flame and nothing but the flame. Think "flame." When you become distracted and other thoughts enter your mind, immediately force your mind back on the flame. Keep looking at the candle. This is your point of focus. Repeat the word "flame" in your mind to help you focus. Every time you do this exercise you are increasing your ability to isolate a thought. You are clearing your mind of chaos. You are strengthening your focus. At first, do this exercise for three minutes. Set a timer if necessary. Eventually, you may do this exercise longer than three minutes. The longer you can keep your mind on the candle, the stronger your ability to focus will become.

It will take time before you are able to focus your mind completely on the flame. Don't get discouraged. With this exercise, we are beginning to learn how to think with the mind and not the brain. The mind is the spiritual part of us. It is not affected by emotions and sensations. At first this exercise may seem difficult. In time it will become easier and then you will find it pleasurable. Your mind will enjoy the harmony of focusing on one thought, the flame, and nothing else. The more often you do this exercise, the better you will learn to isolate a thought. Isolating a thought is the first step toward being able to control your thinking.

Water, Fire, Glass

Floating candles are small candles approximately two inches tall that can float on water. They are widely available in stores. You will need twelve candles to do this exercise. Use a clear glass bowl a minimum of six inches in diameter and three or more inches in height. Fill the bowl with tap water. Put the candles in the bowl of water and light them. Dim the lights in the room or switch them off. Sit somewhere that allows you to gaze down on the bowl. This will create a mystical aura. Here you have the powerful combination of fire, water, and glass. Looking at the candles in the water has a soothing effect and promotes deeper focus. Do not let your thoughts stray from thinking about the candles. If a thought goes in another direction, bring it back. Always think of the word "candles." Do this for ten minutes.

■ GLASS OF WATER

Psychics over time have used water and crystal to help them focus their minds in order to see clear images. Reading a clear crystal ball is a known method for seeing the future. Water has been used as a focal point in order to still the mind. Water has a mystical vibration. The Blessed Virgin Mary has been called the holy mother of the waters. Water has always been linked to a feminine principle. Intuition is a feminine principle. When water is poured into crystal, it has a subtle magnetic force emanating from it. Water and crystal together form a powerful two-fold tool. The first part of this exercise is to isolate a thought; the second is to visualize seeing it done.

Isolate the Thought

In order to obtain anything we want, we must have singleness of purpose. We must first know exactly what we want. We must clear the mind and hold one thought and one thought alone. This is the thought of what we want. It takes training to hold one dominant thought. It takes focus. A glass of water is a remarkable tool to help us focus our minds on one thought and one thought alone.

Choose a clear crystal glass. The glass should be round, such as the type of glass used for wine. The round glass gives it a ball-like shape. Fill the glass with water. Pour the water until it reaches about a quarter inch from the rim of the glass. Place the glass on a table and make certain that the center of the glass is at eye level.

You may put the glass on a book or another type of stand on your table in order to place it high enough to gaze upon it. Sit at the table. You should be sitting at a distance from the glass that is comfortable for you as you focus on the glass of water. Take a deep breath, exhale, and begin to concentrate on the glass of water. Look at the water. Keep your mind focused on the glass of water. Think of the word "water." If your mind wanders, bring it back to the water. Keep taking deep breaths as you continue to focus on the glass of water and nothing but the glass of water. Keep your mind centered on the glass of water.

Do this for two minutes at a time. If you are able to hold the focus on the water longer do so. But two minutes isn't easy. When you are able to focus completely on the word "water" and nothing but water, you have successfully isolated a thought. You may then do the same exercise but replace the word "water' with the thing you most desire. If you want a new job, focus on the words "new job." Look at the glass of water and think only about the new job. Isolate this thought. Keep the mind focused on the glass of water and concentrate on the words "new job." If your mind wanders, bring it back to new job. When we have prepared the mind by focusing on one thing and one thing alone, we are ready to create a picture of this.

Visualize the Thought

The glass of water has now become a tool for visualization. The glass of water will be your screen. Focus your mind on the glass of water. As you focus and concentrate on the glass, begin to create a picture of your specific desire in your mind's eye as you gaze

185

upon the glass of water. Make this a detailed picture of yourself getting what you wish. You will need to use your imagination to form the picture of this. If it is a new job, see how you are dressed to go to work. See the paycheck. See the type of office you will be going to.

Keep your eyes focused on the glass of water. Look at the glass and focus on your picture. It takes practice, but everyone can do this if they repeat it until it works. The potent combination of water and crystal, which has been used to see the future by clairvoyants, can be used by you. You can create the picture of your future. You can see it done. There are many different techniques to employ in order to see a picture of your future. Hold this picture for at least two minutes. Thought needs duration in order to come into the physical world. The longer you can hold a clear picture of your future the faster it will become visible. This takes focus and concentration.

■ PEN AND PAPER

The power of the written word is enormous. The paper can be a focal point. The paper can act like a movie screen. Take a pen and write your goal in capital letters in the middle of the piece of paper. For example, if you want a new house, write NEW HOUSE on the paper. Look at it. Take time to examine this written goal. The written word is denser than mere thought. When you focus the mind on specific words, they will create a picture in your mind. Place this paper somewhere where you can get to it easily. It could be in a side coat pocket, in your purse, or in a drawer that you open often. Look at this paper at least seven times a day. Seven is the number of creation. Every time your mind sees these words, a picture will form in your mind. This repetition will help you to remain focused on your goal. It will also reinforce the thought of your desire in your mind. Repetition is an important element when we are working on manifesting something into our physical life.

If you write something down, you are more aware of it. When you write something down and think about what you wrote down, the thought becomes vitalized. Vital thoughts have longer duration and form more lasting pictures. Thought is energy and form. When we form the words that define a thought, the thought becomes more alive. This will help you to bring the desire into your life more rapidly.

■ OBSERVE YOUR SPEECH

Pick any day of the week and note very carefully the effect your words have on others. Make yourself conscious of the tone of your voice as well as what you are saying. Any time you hear yourself be irritated or short with someone, stop and write this down. Just jot a word or two to remind yourself that you stepped out of balance. Do this for twenty-four hours. This is not an easy exercise, but it has a remarkable effect. It's important to remember that like attracts like in all areas of our life. Any negative thought, word, or action will return a similar one to you. This awareness exercise will help you focus your mind toward harmony.

■ USE THE TELEPHONE TO HELP YOU

When you are trying to form new ways of thinking, you may stumble. It's easy to revert to old habits. Things happen that are disappointing, aggravating, frustrating, and downright annoying. Your thinking gets diverted from your course. Like the people who break their diets and give up because they pigged out at some point, you may abandon your plan to keep your thoughts constructive and focused. Make sure you have someone to phone in case you are diverted from your thinking. Have support in place in case you feel you cannot stay on track. Choose someone who understands what you are doing. It should be someone who also wants to change their way of thinking. Help each other. This is vital, especially when you feel you cannot continue because it's too hard, or it's not working, or it will never happen. Don't wait until you have allowed yourself to go completely negative. At the mere hint of giving up, pick up the phone. We all need support. You do not have to do this alone. The telephone is a lifeline. It works.

Thought is
    the creative power
      in the universe

five

USING THE POWER
OF THOUGHT
TO GET WHAT
YOU WANT

We all want the same things. It is within our human nature to desire the things that can make us feel safe, comfortable, and happy. There is nothing wrong with living a comfortable life. In fact, a life that is secure could leave a person more time to pursue the spiritual side of life. The less time pursuing our physical needs, the more left for contemplating the spiritual. When a person is healthy, financially stable, passionate in a secure personal relationship, keenly interested in their work, and happy, he or she is more likely to have time to spend on things that bring greater harmony.

How many times do you hear that someone didn't have time to meditate, listen to beautiful music, practice his or her thinking, or visit a sick friend? When we are freed from the stress of fighting an illness, paying the bills, working on our personal life, or securing a fulfilling job, the time will be there.

When we live in a state of harmony, we have found happiness. This state of harmony can only be achieved through a conscious shift in our thinking. Everything that we are doing in this book is leading us toward a more balanced life full of goodness. A conscious change in our everyday attitude is life altering. When we allow the Divine Force to work through us, we manifest things with the least amount of trouble.

Some people must focus on their health before they can focus on anything else. Others feel they must stabilize their finances first. And there are those who cannot live without a happy personal life. Many people that I meet are desperate to find the perfect job. And there are some who say, "I just want to be happy."

First and foremost, it is absolutely essential that you decide what it is that you want most. You may want many things. This is fine. But one thing at a time must

be your motto. Once you decide what you want most, you must see yourself having it. You cannot vacillate. Keep your focus on your goal. See a clear picture of yourself getting what you want. From the moment you wake up until you go to sleep, you must remain aware of your thinking. Don't go negative. Keep your thoughts in harmony with the Divine Force. Find quiet time to focus on the picture of your goal. The more often you visualize your goal the faster it will come into form.

■ PREPARATION

We should prepare both ourselves and our physical surroundings in order to perform the visualization exercises most effectively. We don't need specific hours, but we do need blocks of time every day that are dedicated to learning how to focus our thoughts. Once we have learned to focus, we can then train ourselves to see ourselves clearly having what we want. The visualizations of the exact goal may take only a few minutes. But it takes time to relax. It's hard to let go of the tensions that are part of everyday life. Therefore, I suggest that fifteen minutes at least three times a day be set aside for training.

Preparation means that we choose the proper place

for our mental homework. It should be a place where we feel good and where we will not be interrupted. Some people have a special room in their house. Others just find a quiet corner. If traveling, choose the best possible place you can find. But we must make this the most important thing in our day. When you have finished your visualization, let it go and go back to your normal activities. Keep your thinking positive. This type of thinking will make everything in your life easier.

Here is a helpful tool that will keep your thinking on an elevated level. Any time you have a free moment, focus on the Divine Force. You just say the words "Divine Force" in your mind. Keep saying "Divine Force" with a reverent attitude. Why don't you focus on the Divine Force while you are making the coffee, waiting for the train, standing in line at the grocery store, riding in an elevator, picking up the kids, or during your lunch break? This focus will keep your thinking on the right track. You will feel centered.

■ YOU WILL BE TESTED

When you start using your thought in the right way, you will be tested. Thoughts of defeat will try to enter your mind. Don't allow them in. For example, you desire a certain amount of money. You have a clear picture in your mind of yourself getting this money. You visualize three times a day and clearly see the amount of money coming into your life. Then you find yourself unable to pay your bills. This causes you to think you are being foolish. You believe this is not going to happen and you will never get the money. You lose faith. All you see is failure. You must force your mind to stop immediately seeing the picture of failure and replace it with the picture of getting the money you need. Take a deep breath, and ask the Divine Force to help you. Choose an amount of money that seems realistic and see the money coming from an honorable source. Do something constructive to help this to come about.

Steve, a manufacturer of pillows, received his desired money by landing a huge new account. His business was in a lot of trouble. He needed financial help fast. This new account came out of the blue. He'd never done business with a major chain store. He never thought of pursuing this kind of account. Steve learned to focus. He made a conscious effort to have a positive attitude. He followed the rules and went to work with a new optimism. Steve found that as he focused on his thought he felt better about everything in his life. His mood changed from nervous and short-tempered to calm and more tolerant. He focused on the Divine Force often, always before he left for work and the last thing at night. Steve worked extra hard to help make this money come into the business. He kept his thought focused on his goal until he reached it. Steve continues to work on developing new habits of right thinking. He has shared his knowledge about thought with his employees.

Let me add an important detail about visualizations. When you are creating the picture of what you want, don't limit yourself. For example, if you want a husband, don't see only one specific person even if you are dating someone at the time. Keep your options open. Yes, your current love may become your spouse. But it's possible that the universe may present you with someone better. Just picture yourself at your wedding. See yourself looking happy, beautiful, and in love. Remember, there are many possibilities waiting for you.

Do anything that you can do to help your desire come into being. Let's say you need a new job. After you finish your meditation exercise, proceed to do something constructive. Any action that puts you in a place that might help you attract the new job is useful. Sending your résumé, making phone calls, reading the job section of the newspaper are practical steps that

may help your job manifest. You never know exactly where the answer will come from. Keep an open mind and stay alert. The answer will come.

We will now work with six of the most common desires that people of all walks of life seek. We will use the rules and the tools to show how these can be achieved by using our thought in the right way.

■ 1. HEALTH

Many people do not understand how thought and health are linked. People can see how thoughts properly controlled can bring a car, a house, a job, money, or a love affair to them. But they have yet to understand how thought brings health or disease as well. All illness and all wellness are equally the result of the way we think. Thoughts and feelings affect our emotional bodies and create vibrations of harmony or disharmony. This in turn affects the physical body.

When we keep our thoughts constructive, centered, kind, and loving, we are happy. Happiness brings harmony. Living in harmony creates health. Disease is the result of living in disharmony. Anger, anxiety, frustration, disappointment, worry, and stress create thought forms that break down the physical body. When these negative thought forms are too strong, the body is depleted of vital force. We lack sufficient energy to release the negative thought forms and replace them with harmonious ones. Whenever we are sick or injured, we create a picture of the problem in our mind. If we focus on this picture over and over, it can be very difficult to get rid of it.

Peter

Peter was in a car accident and suffered a painful neck injury. He went to a number of doctors, who prescribed nerve and pain medications. These drugs gave him a little relief, but the pain continued. He had x-rays, an MRI, and ultrasound tests, which revealed that the pain should not be so severe. But Peter's pain did not go away. He went to physical therapy two times a week, had massage therapy, and acupuncture. But the pain did not let up.

Peter came for an appointment hoping that I could see that his problem would be resolved. Peter related the story of his injury to me. He kept repeating that his neck hurt. I could see that as he said, "My neck hurts," anxiety was building up.

Peter added, "I keep telling myself to think that my

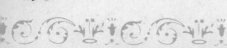

neck does not hurt. I read somewhere that you need to put the thought of the opposite in your head in order to make something negative go away."

"Peter, every time you think about your neck problem, be it thinking 'it hurts' or thinking 'it does not hurt' you are flashing the picture of your injured neck in your mind. This intensifies the pain because the repetition of the picture is strengthening the thought form. You are what you think. It is necessary to stop and change the picture in your mind. But the new picture must not be related to your neck at all. Every time you allow your mind to think about the neck problem, you are giving it force, energy, and power. I want you to focus your thinking on the Divine Force. Everything good—health, strength, and balance—comes from the Divine Force. The Divine Force has no health problems. I want you to take a deep breath, close your eyes, and focus your thought on the Divine Force. Whenever the picture of the pain in your neck flashes in your mind, replace this thought with the words 'Divine Force.' Continue your treatment knowing that the Divine Force is working through you. Do whatever you can to help in any way possible to resolve your problem. But do not allow your mind to dwell on your neck."

Peter agreed to give it a try. Six months later, Peter returned to see me. His neck was almost back to normal. Once in a while he still had some pain, but if this happened he would think about the Divine Force and not his neck. He was amazed at how much this helped him.

"Apparently," Peter said to me, "everybody noticed a change. It was interesting how my physical therapist and the acupuncturist commented that I seemed to be doing surprisingly better."

Peter is an example of the power that thought has over our health. He was fortunate that he was able to rid himself of his pain quickly. This is not always the case.

Did you ever wonder why one person catches a contagious disease and another does not? When people hear that there is a disease floating around, they get worried and continuously think about catching it, "Oh, my God, I might get it." They see a picture in their minds of the full-blown disease. They repeat the picture over and over. It's not long before the fear and stress of worrying about it brings it on.

Sometimes we catch things even when we were not consciously thinking or worrying about them. The common cold and flu are examples. Most everyone has had these. Many times these are brought upon us because our immune system is weakened as a result of emotional stress. The root cause of our emotional stress can be found in our thinking. When a thought is held for a prolonged period it will manifest. Any thought or emotion held and repeated will bring an equal result. Anger, hatred, bitterness, resentment, envy, and jealousy create powerful thought forms and always result in either a physical or mental malady. It could take a day, a week, a month, a year, or thirty years for the individual to see definite results in the physical body. But they will be seen.

Our thinking has an enormous affect on our health. A healthy diet, taking vitamins, exercising, and not smoking or abusing alcohol will help you remain healthy. But it takes right thinking, discipline, motivation, and will power to adhere to this lifestyle. Good health begins with our thinking.

Sometimes we must live with an illness our entire lives. There are other times when the illness can be resolved while we have time to enjoy life without it. Prolonged anxiety is often the root of a serious illness. The only hope for a cure is to rid ourselves of the negative thoughts that caused the anxious state of mind.

Becky

Becky came to see me because she was unhappy in her marriage. There was not one thing about her husband that she could tolerate. He was not making enough money, their sex life was terrible, he never complimented her, never picked up his clothes, and never helped with the dishes or any household chores. He would always side with their daughter against her. In all my years of professional work I had rarely met anyone this miserable in a marriage who was not planning to get a divorce. I observed Becky as I listened to her rant; I saw in her aura a deep-rooted kindness. But the angry feelings toward her husband were taking over, almost like some kind of possession.

"I don't want a divorce. I want him to change." She started to cry.

"You can't change the way someone else behaves. You can only change yourself. Becky, you will remain miserable, or worse, it could affect your health if you don't change your thinking."

"What about his thinking?" she snapped. "He is the

one who has to change." Then she began another tirade.

Three years passed before Becky returned to see me. She had been diagnosed with breast cancer, which had been caught in time. She had treatment, one breast was removed, and the cancer went into remission. When I saw her, it was about six months after the reconstruction surgery.

She looked wonderful. Becky had always taken good care of herself. She lived a healthy lifestyle. She was thin and exercised religiously, not only aerobic but also yoga. She took vitamins and always had yearly medical checkups. No wonder Becky had been shocked when she was diagnosed with cancer. After she updated me, she immediately started complaining about her husband. I could see that she was right back to where we had left off in our first session. Becky had not been able to stop fuming about her husband's shortcomings. I asked her if he had been supportive during her cancer treatments.

She said, "Well, he drove me, picked me up, and took me to my treatments."

I did not know what to say. She apparently had no idea how destructive her thoughts were. She had not been able to implement any change in her thinking. I tried again to reach her and strongly advised her to make a conscious effort to change her thinking from destructive to constructive. I feared her health would suffer. We spent an hour discussing what was harmful in her thinking. When she left that day, she said, "I understand that I have to change my thinking."

After that I received a few phone calls from Becky. She had been able to stop complaining about her husband. It took a great effort for her to do this. She had asked a friend to help her to change the way she thought about her husband. She is still in remission.

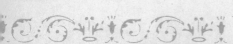

It is common to hear that someone's heart attack was the result of too much stress. Many other ailments, some types of cancer, skin problems, alopecia, stomach ulcers, back pain, and headaches, to name just a few, are often found to be rooted in stressful lifestyles as well.

You may be thinking, "Good luck trying to live a stress-free life on this planet."

We may not be able to eliminate the anxieties and pressures that are part of our world, but we can decide how to cope with them. I just flew back to New York from London. The security at Heathrow airport, which already was intense because of 9/11, had been increased as a result of new terrorist threats. The lines were taking close to two hours. People were exhausted, angry, confused, and some were frightened. The airport was a pressure cooker.

One man in front of me became enraged when he was not allowed to use a special lane reserved for first class passengers on British Airways. He had been first class on another airline and believed he should be able to go through the special lane. Not only was he refused access to the fast lane, a security woman forced him to pick up his hand luggage, which he was pulling on wheels, because the hand luggage had to be "carry-on." He started to flip out. He was reined in when I pointed out to him a sign posted on the wall that said, "Verbal abuse or any type of violence against security personnel will be prosecuted to the full extent of the law." This made him stop and think for a moment. I could see that it was difficult for him, but he chose to focus on getting through the security check. And thankfully he did.

There were other people who seemed short-tempered, put out, and exasperated. There were some

who seemed to be taking it with a grain of salt. They were not bothered by the hassle. The pressure did not stop once I got through security. Waiting for my flight I was bombarded by the angry, fearful thought forms permeating in the terminal. The vibration was awful. It was a great relief to me finally to board the plane.

But I was aware of the thought forms of fear that were pulsating through the cabin. I read and meditated until we reached cruising altitude. This helped me to remain in harmony until I could take out my CD player and listen to Mozart. The music had an immediate calming effect. Once again Mozart was the perfect prescription for relieving anxiety. I only wished I could have piped the music throughout the whole cabin.

Travel has become increasingly stressful, forcing people to learn ways to handle it. How many of us have found ourselves sick after returning home from air travel? Some think this is because the cabin air is toxic. That may be true, but I still believe that stress is the major factor. Meditation and Mozart's music are two of the most potent yet simple methods for dealing with the anxiety connected with travel.

Thought and Well-Being

Thank goodness the medical profession is beginning to accept the enormous role our minds play in our overall well-being. Many professionals are prescribing treatments that have healing effects on the mind and body. Meditation, yoga, breathing exercises, massage therapy, acupressure, acupuncture, and supplements, to name a few, are no longer perceived by many as "alternative" or "new age." They are being used more and more because the positive effects are becoming clearer. These treatments promote harmony and help to produce balance. Balance and harmony generate a feeling of overall well-being. All health is a result of harmonious thinking and living.

Bedside Manner

How many people could be helped by a kind word from a doctor? My clients have told me too often about their frustration upon leaving their doctors' offices. They report that the doctor was rushed, abrupt, or that they were left waiting or could not get in to see him at all. Many people give up when they are told by a doctor they have little or no chance of recovery. On the other hand, some people refuse to hear that the medical profession has become extremely demanding. The high costs of running a medical practice leaves the physicians little time to give individual attention to patients.

I am not a medical doctor, nor do I ever suggest that a client come to me for a diagnosis or prescriptions instead of seeing their personal physician. But one out of every two people has a health problem. Some are minor like a cold every winter or a slight allergy; others are deadly serious. Even if I see a terminal illness, I can help the person deal with the fear, anxiety, torment, pain, and anger.

The first thing I do is to tell them not to be hard on themselves. We cannot change the past; we can only deal with the present and the future.

People should focus on something that makes them happy. It could be a weekend with their beloved, an evening at the opera, dinner at their favorite restaurant, or a visit from an old friend. They must see themselves enjoying any one of these activities.

Laurie

Laurie, a friend of mine, has breast cancer. This is her second bout. She believed she was cured. So, it was a terrible shock when her checkup showed the cancer had returned. She had surgery and is now undergoing chemotherapy and radiation.

Laurie is remarkable. I am humbled by her grace, courage, and humor as she battles this terrible disease. I asked her how she was keeping up her spirits. She turned to me and said, "You ought to know," making a joke because I am a psychic. But she smiled and said, "Mary, you taught me about the power of thought years ago. Do you think I have forgotten now, just when I need it the most? When it gets really difficult, I ask the Divine Force to help me find the best way to cope with my illness. This calms me and helps me to center my thinking. I have faith in my doctor, who has also become a friend. I know that many other people have faced similar or more difficult challenges and this too gives me courage."

Laurie continues to live with hope and humor even though the treatments cause her to be exhausted and nauseous. She removes the image of the illness from her mind and replaces it with pictures of health and harmony. This is a type of meditation she practices many times a day. Whenever she feels up to it, she goes to a movie, a play, or meets friends for dinner. These types of activities promote balance and help to keep her mind focused on life-affirming actions. She never feels sorry for herself. All of her friends, me included, always feel better for having spent time with her. No one is ever at a loss for words, because she makes all of us feel comfortable. Laurie is very aware of the reactions that people can have to a person who has cancer. She is determined to help her family and friends deal with her illness. This makes everybody passionate to help her in any way possible. Even her boss will do anything to make her life easier. He allows her to work when she is able to and never makes her feel insecure about her job. Laurie is an inspiration for all of us. As of now, she is doing very well. Laurie takes one day at a time and enjoys every one of them.

■ 2. GREAT SEX

There is a misconception by some people that great sex is dependent on physical appearance alone. Many men and women are obsessed by this idea. Magazines, movies, television, and billboards project images of how we are supposed to look in order to be sexually attractive. This focus on physical appearance can make people feel undesired and insignificant. The perfect body does not guarantee great sex. Often people with perfect looks are that way because they spend all their time thinking about themselves and the way they look. Haven't you heard the story of Narcissus? He saw his reflection in a pool of water and fell in love with himself. He wasted away looking at himself. When all our thoughts are focused on ourselves, there is no energy left to think about making a partner happy in bed.

Jake

Jake wanted someone who looked like a sex symbol. This was the key to his happiness. I told Jake that he could have this. He would need to believe that it was possible. He should visualize himself being in bed with a woman who looked like what he had in mind. He should do this at least three times a day. He then should let the picture go. Thoughts and ideas suggesting places to go, people to call, or things to do that will make this happen will come into his mind. He must act on them. Impatience could ruin this. Persistence pays off. Jake wrote everything down as I

211

said it. He then read my instructions back to me to make certain he got it right.

1. I must believe I can have this.

2. I must picture myself in bed.

3. I must do this at least three times a day.

4. I then have to let this picture go.

5. Ideas will come to me telling me things to do and people to call.

6. I must act on them.

7. I can't be impatient because persistence pays off.

After our session he went home and that very day started picturing himself in bed with this sexy, perfect woman. He saw this picture over and over. It became more and more detailed. This exercise was easy for him.

It didn't take discipline to see his sexual fantasy come into being. But getting it from his mind to his bedroom took a little work. One day he was working out at his gym and started talking to one of the trainers. Jake asked the trainer if he knew where he could meet women with this type of look.

The trainer said, "You are at the wrong New York City gym. You need to join Equinox on East Fifty-seventh Street. That's where you will find these hot women. They all work out there."

It had never dawned on Jake that he was at the wrong gym if he wanted to meet sexy women. The next day he became a member of Equinox. Shortly after, in a yoga class, he met a gorgeous, 36D blond, perfect body and asked her out. They went to a night club. The atmosphere was sexually charged. They danced until the club closed and ended up in bed.

"It worked, didn't it, Jake? You followed the rules and got what you wanted."

"What I thought I wanted," he said. "The sex was okay, but I felt disappointed. I thought I would feel on top of the world, but the sex was not satisfying. I felt I was with a store mannequin. She was beautiful, with a great body, but she didn't have any passion. She was more worried that she would break a fingernail than anything else. We didn't talk much. But the few words she said were about her workouts and her diet. It was boring. I was glad when I left her apartment and went home."

"Why did you want to see me today? It can't be only to tell me that you got what you wanted by using your thinking?"

"I thought you could tell me how to do it better. I must have done something wrong because the sex wasn't great."

"Jake, when are you going to wake up and smell the coffee? What you think you want does not always make you happy. There is nothing wrong with wanting to have a terrific sex life. The mistake was in believing that a great body alone would be enough to make this happen. You have to have feelings for the person with the great body in order to have wonderful sex. They have to have feelings for you as well. It takes two."

Martha

Martha is overweight, does not care much for clothes, never goes to the beauty parlor, doesn't make a lot of money, but has the best sex life of anybody I have ever met. Men love Martha. She is a great conversationalist, a great listener, and she sees herself as sexy. She told me that when she was younger she had low self-esteem. Luckily, she had fallen in love with an older man who made her feel attractive and desirable. He had taught her that she must always think of herself as wonderful.

"You are only as good as you think you are," he told her.

These words stayed with Martha. She is able to make other people feel good as well. Martha loves making her lovers feel wonderful. She is a living example that one does not have to possess the perfect body in order to have great sex. She has a depth of feeling that transcends the physical body. This makes her very attractive. She feels sorry for women who starve themselves and believe they are not sexy unless they look like cover girls. Martha's way of thinking should inspire all of us.

There are women who spend fortunes having their bodies nipped and tucked hoping this will make them more sexually desirable. Some will do anything in order to look younger, thinner, or more toned. The business

215

of plastic surgery is so dominant on the minds of people that there are now hit television shows based on it. Plastic surgeons have become celebrities writing books and marketing their "beauty products" on television and in magazines.

Everywhere we turn, the message seems to be that you can never look good enough, young enough, or appealing enough. "If you use Botox, your lips will be kissable. If you enhance your breasts, men will be dropping at your feet. If you do your eyes, you will look ten years younger. With liposuction (any part of the body, it doesn't matter) you will instantly, without laborious dieting and exercise, have a sought-after body. You can fix any part of yourself (even the parts that used to be termed unthinkable) in order to be more sexually attractive." The reality is that those who think this way will never be happy.

Anne

I met Anne in an acting class in 1978. Perky and cute, Anne had enormous talent but never believed in herself. As I got to know her, I was amazed by the self-hatred that dominated her thinking. She felt fat. No amount of dieting would make her feel she was thin enough. Anne could sing like an angel, dance like a

Rockette, and act like Sarah Bernhard but this did not help her to feel confident about herself. It was not only her body she hated, she had her nose fixed, her breasts implanted, and her teeth capped before she was thirty. In her need for constant confirmation she had numerous one-night stands, always believing that these sexual encounters would lead to long-term relationships. In fact, they merely left her feeling lonely and rejected.

Anne did not try to examine her behavior from an emotional or spiritual point of view. She believed that these affairs ended because she was not sexually desirable enough. All of her friends, myself included, spent copious amounts of time trying to convince her that she was a terrific person with great looks. Our words landed on deaf ears. As time went on, she became more and more emotionally unstable because of her obsession with her looks. Anne continued to seek the confirmation she desired through having empty sexual encounters. In time she became completely anorexic and this led to other medical problems. Sadly, there was no longer any sign of the perky, talented actress whom I had known. I was told by a mutual acquaintance that to this day Anne continues with her obsession.

■

Many people do not see the connection between sex and having a relationship. They think that sex can be fulfilling on its own. This may work for a short while. But ultimately, sex needs a relationship.

Dave

Dave, an accountant, arrived for his appointment looking depressed. He had ended another relationship. It had seemed very promising at the beginning. She was the most beautiful woman he had ever met. She dressed perfectly for the clubs and bars he took her to. At first sex with her was exciting. Several months later, however, he felt that their sex life had become routine. He became less attracted to her. Finally, they stopped seeing each other.

He did not understand why this kept happening to him. I told him he had to start by changing his thinking. He should try to get to know the person before he goes to bed with her. Talk to the person. Connect. Spend time together. This is the only way to develop feelings. As these feelings grow, the sex will follow, and it will be great sex. Dave was confused because he never thought about this. Dave now has a happy personal relationship. It took him over a year to implement his new way of thinking. But he now understands what it means to have a great sex life.

■

Good sex begins in the mind. It is rooted in a meeting of the minds. This meeting like any meeting begins with conversation. In fact, the better the conversation the better the mutual understanding. This mutual exchange leads to an emotional connection. This connection is fueled by energy and produces deeper feelings. The results are immediate. Instead of just sex, people can have great sex. A meeting of the minds may take some time. It may take getting together with many different people. You must not get discouraged. Persistence pays off. You must begin somewhere.

■ 3. MONEY

Money is a symbol of value in our world. Most people prize it more than anything else. Every client in the last twenty-five years has asked at least one question about money. Many people simply want to know if they will ever be rich. The rich ask if they will remain that way or if they will get richer. Everyone is burdened by money in one way or another. There is nothing inherently wrong with wanting money. But a life devoted completely to the accumulation of money will leave a person empty. Thinking "prosperity" day and night can be very exhausting. We are born into the physical, material world to learn and grow. Money is a part of that growth. It is a great test for all of us. Money in and of itself isn't the root of all evil. It's the selfish, do-anything desire to get it that can become evil.

We need to examine the way we think about money. First, there are three ways to acquire money. We are born with it, earn it, or get it by external circumstances. The third way could be inheritance, or even a lottery. Which way applies to you?

The soul isn't measured by possessions. The soul is measured by the way it handles possessions. Everywhere we look, everywhere we turn, our thinking is focused on the need for more and more money. Maybe you have seen or read one of the many bestselling books that tell us that even "God wants us to be rich." Of course, it is wise to focus our thought to acquire money with less effort. The energy and focus it takes to make money leaves us little leisure time. There is little time for the things that promote harmony. Spending time with our families, feeling fitter, gaining knowledge, relaxing, loving, and learning are examples of this. So we are unhappy and unbalanced and feel that things would have been okay if we just had more money.

How many relationships are plagued by quarrels over money? Money can trigger jealousy, cause ulcers, corruption, and nervous breakdowns. On the other hand, the proper and balanced use of money can bring freedom. Money can reduce our stress when we have enough to pay our bills.

No matter how we analyze it, money is on our minds.

Lester

Lester first came to see me in 1986. He was twenty-three years old and had been given a session with me by his sister for his birthday. He and his sister were very close, having lost both their parents within the last ten years. At the time of our meeting, Lester had a job at a warehouse packing books. He was making around eighteen thousand dollars a year working long hours and

overtime. There was something about Lester that was extremely likeable. He vibrated a kindness and calmness that one does not usually see in someone that young. He had lovely manners that seemed as if he had been born in a different era.

Lester told me he wanted to be rich, very rich. He said this with certainty and asked me: "How do you see me doing this?"

I started to laugh, because it sounded as if he just needed directions from my office to the subway station while in fact he was asking for a roadmap to wealth. "Lester, how fast do you have to be very rich, and, what does very rich mean to you?"

"I am willing to work hard and I have patience. I want at least twenty million dollars. That's my idea of being very rich."

"Yes, that's very rich. We better get started."

I knew that Lester would be able to fulfill his desire. But I also saw this was not going to be easy and that it would take longer than Lester imagined. His patience would be greatly tested, because it would take twenty years. So, I said, "Lester, I predict you will do this but it will take a while. You will have many jobs that lead to your goal. You will travel." I went on to tell him what the process would entail.

Lester listened intently and asked me if he could take notes. He picked up the pen and paper and wrote down a few things, then asked, "Where do you see me traveling?"

"One place is very, very cold. You will need clothes that you don't have yet. In another place, I see you are wearing beach clothes and living on the water. It looks like a Carribean island, I don't know which one. There could be another place in between. But I see that one job leads you to the next and to the next in your quest to become wealthy."

"You just said it depends upon my thinking. What do you mean; what do I have to do?"

I proceeded to instruct him on the rules of thinking. I stressed that he could not just sit at home and think himself rich. He would need to take action. It would take physical work as well as disciplined thinking.

Twenty years passed and I heard from Lester. It was recently in fact. He called wanting to make an appointment to see me. It took me a minute to remember who he was after all these years. He walked in very tanned and was dressed impeccably with understated elegance.

"Do you remember that you predicted that I would be back to see you when I was very rich?" he asked me.

"Yes, I do, Lester, and I see that you indeed have made your fortune."

He sat down and told me how it all happened. He had left the session that day and immediately started a conscious effort to implement what I had taught him. He visualized himself being very rich at least five times a day. When he began, it was hard to hold the picture of his goal longer than a few seconds. But he persisted in practicing until he was able to produce a clear picture in his mind's eye at will. This took more than a few years to achieve. At first he had to be in a physical place where he would visualize with no interruption and he would only be able to see the picture with his eyes closed. It was hard to stop other thoughts that were not part of the picture coming in, but persistence paid off.

Six months after our first session, he was at work at the warehouse and it was a dinner break. He was in the cafeteria and someone asked if he could share the table as the cafeteria was packed. His name was Pete and he had just gotten a job at the warehouse. Over time they would run into each other and became friendly. Pete told Lester about his brother, who had gone to Alaska to work on the oil pipeline and was making a lot of money.

"What kind of money" Lester asked Pete.

224

"Over fifty thousand dollars a year."

"Why don't you go there to make all that money?"

"It's too cold. I could not take it. Sometimes my brother wakes up and there are icicles hanging off his beard. You would not believe the stories of how hard it is. But the money is great."

"How do you get a job there?"

"I will get in touch with my brother. Sometimes it takes a few days before he is near a phone. But I will ask him when I reach him."

A week passed when Pete came up to Lester: "I got the number. This is whom you should contact if you want a job on the pipeline."

Lester had been working more overtime in the warehouse but did not feel that there was any future in it. He called the next day. Within two weeks he had signed up and was packing to leave for Alaska. When he was on the airplane going to Alaska he remembered my prediction. I had told him one of the jobs leading to his fortune would be in a place that was very cold.

The job was brutal. He did not know how he made it through the first week. The temperatures were frigid, the accommodations awful, the food inedible, and he was lonely. But he could make a lot of money and put it away. He continued his visualizations.

Though it was difficult, he kept the faith. Three years passed and he had saved a good sum. He was thinking about his next move. He didn't want to stay in Alaska any longer, but he didn't know where to go. He could not take the cold and loneliness anymore. He was exhausted but remained strong in his belief that he would be very rich in the future. Where could he go; what could he do?

He went to Anchorage on his day off and stopped by a restaurant for something to eat. He started talking to the waitress. Her name was Sally. They talked for a while and during the conversation Lester told Sally that he was ready to leave Alaska and needed to find a well-paying job. That's when she told him that her brother- in-law owned a construction company in the Chicago area.

"Have you ever done construction?" she asked him.

Lester answered, "No, but I have strong muscles having worked on the pipeline. I believe I can do that."

That's how Lester ended up in Chicago. With the money he had saved in Alaska, he bought a run-down building with another guy from the construction crew. They were able to fix up the building. Two years later, Lester doubled his money. He finally began to feel that real wealth was getting closer.

He continued his meditations and stayed alert to possibilities that could guide him to his goal. Since he had learned how to renovate and sell small buildings successfully, he did several more renovation projects— buying, renovating, and selling the buildings. He was close to having his first million.

He had not had a vacation for ten years. When his sister asked him to go on a cruise with her to the Caribbean islands, he agreed to go with her. When the cruise ship docked at one of the islands, Lester met a beautiful young woman named Chloe and fell for her. He decided to stay on the island. She was a painter and was selling her paintings in a small gift shop on the island. She was also working in a restaurant. Her shop gave Lester an idea. He saw the possibility of having a shop on the island. It would be good for his girlfriend as well. She could have her paintings displayed and also work there. She would no longer have to waitress. He put the word out and talked to everyone that he wanted to buy a shop. Chloe talked to everyone she met at the restaurant. Within six months, Lester had his shop. Because he had been in construction, Lester was able to fix up the shop beautifully. They also started to have an incredible line of artistic T-shirts that Chloe had designed. These took off and sold as fast as they could produce them. Lester told me: "The store turned out to be a money magnet."

"Well, Lester, like attracts like."

He laughed and told me that he then created a chain of stores throughout most of the islands around him and was even shipping to Europe. He married Chloe. They have two daughters. Lester was in New York because he had just completed a deal where he sold his chain of stores to a conglomerate.

"Mary, in 1986, you told me that if I could *see it done* I could make it happen. Do you remember that during our session you told me that I would travel and work in different places? One of the places you predicted would be very cold and another place you said looked like the Caribbean. And there was a third place in between but you didn't know where. Well, you were right. It took twenty years, but I just closed the deal for the sale of the shops and I will net over twenty million."

Lester was extraordinarily grateful. He said he wished that everyone could understand how important thought was. He always shared what I told him about using thought to get what you want in life. He felt he had helped some people. He wasn't certain what his next move would be, but he was looking forward to spending time with his girls. He knew if he kept his thinking on the right track the next opportunity would present itself. He had absolute faith in that.

■

It took Lester twenty years to get what he wanted. He told me he wanted twenty million dollars and I told him how to get it. He did the work. He had the will. He kept the faith. He persisted until he had reaped the results that he desired. He still vibrated the same kindness and calmness that I saw in him at the age of twenty-three. His wealth had not changed his character. I could see that he was going to do great things with his money and have a lot of fun spending it.

Of course, not everyone will make twenty million dollars. Many people are able to use the power of thought to help them take care of their immediate needs; others are able to avert a financial crisis. Many people have been able to save their business at the eleventh hour, which demanded extreme focus, exceptional faith, and tremendous discipline. Others were able to improve their standard of living nicely.

Lois

One friend of mine, Lois, is an excellent graphic de-signer who was terrified of retiring because she had little savings. I told her she had to focus her thinking on getting some money quickly and I gave her these steps. She had to see herself looking at her retirement portfolio. She must see the amount of money needed in order to retire safely. I explained visualization and told her the more details she could envision the better. De-tails help us to have increased faith. The clearer a pic-ture can be seen in our minds the more quickly it can be brought into our physical world. Lois visualized her retirement fund five times a day.

I said, "Lois, why so often?"

"Because I am having my fiftieth birthday and I have to get this together now."

"You always were an overachiever!" I stressed that she needed a positive attitude in everything she did.

Because of the nature of her work, Lois had great concentration skills. She could focus better than almost anyone I knew. Lois enjoyed her visualization sessions. I suggested that she could also use Mozart's music and this would have an added benefit. Lois was thrilled to try this out. I told her any Mozart music that she really enjoyed could be useful. Lois found that the visualization and Mozart's music made her feel inspired. She increased her effort to attract new clients. She sent out a huge mailing and made appointments with new potential accounts. Her enhanced sense of faith was magnetic. She brought in new business at an accelerated rate. She was enjoying her work more than ever and this also affected her business. People wanted to do business with somebody who was so positive and creative. Lois found herself playing Mozart all the time. Ideas came to her more easily. It did not take long before she saw the financial results as well. Lois is well on her way to retire with a sense of security.

People's money reality differs greatly. Jean, a woman whom I met years ago, is perfectly happy living on the pension she has from her job as a postal worker. She has few desires and loves not going to work. She feels blessed that she has this stable income.

Leonard is a multimillionaire who is consumed with keeping his lifestyle. He has homes in Manhattan, East Hampton, and Florida. But even this is not enough. Leonard wants more money. He wants a private jet. I told him that was fine and suggested he keep focusing on more money and he'd have it.

John would be happy if he were free of credit card debt. He lives in fear of going bankrupt. Each of these people views money differently, but they all want what they perceive to be enough to live the way they want. In today's world, money is also a needed tool for our spiritual growth. We develop character traits by the way we handle money. When we die, we take our thoughts but not our money. There are no banks on the other side. I had a very wealthy client come for a session. He wanted to know if I could tell him when and where he would be born in his next life so that he could leave his money to himself.

Claudia

Claudia had been to every seminar, lecture, class, and workshop and bought every book known to man, all on the subject of manifesting money. She arrived at her appointment to see me still looking for the magic answer to the age-old question of how to make a great deal of money. Nothing she'd tried before had worked.

Looking at her I realized that the issue was life and death for her. She lacked faith. I told her to stop running around in circles. She was dissipating her energy and not focusing on her goal. She must use the power of thought to help bring the money into her life. She must *see it done.* She must create the picture of herself being very rich. As she went about her life, she would find that opportunities for making money would become apparent. I stressed that faith was the essential ingredient for making this happen. She must have complete belief in her ability to get the money. But thought alone is not enough. It must be followed by actions. Claudia must do anything in her power to make her thought become a reality in her world.

Two years later, Claudia came back to see me. She had followed my advice to the letter. An unexpected bonus at work was the first sign that things were working. She took the bonus money, invested it in an Internet company whose stock quadrupled within a year. She is well on her way to being a rich woman.

■

There is an important lesson here. How many times have you met someone who has achieved something that appeared to be impossible? If you asked them how they did it, there is one consistent answer. They believed they could.

233

■ 4. THE PERFECT JOB

People who are unhappy with their work are miserable. Depression, lethargy, weight gain, office romances, anger, and envy are just some of the symptoms of the "not having the perfect job" syndrome. I cannot tell you how many people have come to see me over the years because they could not find a job that was fulfilling and paid the bills at the same time.

Think about how many hours of your life are spent in your workplace. It's obvious that the need to find work that you enjoy is paramount to overall happiness.

Many people need self-expression—artistic, literary, or otherwise. The need for this type of work is strong in these people. If this is not accomplished, people feel as if they are living half a life.

Jack

A client of mine just got a job in the theater. He is fifty-one and had always dreamed of acting. But he never could find the way toward fulfilling his goal.

When Jack first came to see me it was two years before this theater job was acquired. He was in a state of despair. Jack was teaching part-time at a small college, was always short on cash, and had overspent with credit cards. His knees were causing him a lot of pain and he had gotten out of shape because he was having trouble exercising. He was riddled with problems.

It was difficult to decide which problem I should focus on first. There was a kindness in this man that was vibrating underneath the thoughts of his unhappiness. The only time I saw his aura lift was when I spoke about the theater. He reminded me of the actor Spencer Tracey, and I could see him playing similar roles that Spencer Tracey played.

I asked which of his problems he thought should first be tackled. He said, "Well, it will have to be money. I can't even take an acting class unless I have some money. I am in debt. I have a job that does not pay enough and all I have ever wanted all my life was to be an actor."

I said, "Jack, we better get the money, because once you have a bit of financial security your thought will be free to focus on the theater."

I told him that he must see himself being able to pay his bills and have enough left over to take an acting class. I said he should picture himself looking calm and at ease, because he can take care of his debts. He must see himself writing checks for bills or paying them

235

online, however he chooses to see himself financially stable. He had taken meditation classes when he was younger, which had taught him how to focus. Because he was in his heart an actor, it was easy for him to understand what it meant to do creative visualization. He loved the thought of seeing himself in a role. His role was playing a sixty-year-old man who did not have money problems. This role also included the man leaving his home on his way to an acting class that would result in a job in the theater.

Jack became so excited at the thought of doing this role that he told me he could see what he was wearing in his role. He would wear gray wool pants with a white shirt that had a slight gray stripe through it that would match the pants. He paused for a moment and then added a tie to the outfit. Jack was on his way. I discussed with him that it was necessary to do this visualization at least twice a day and to hold the picture for at least two minutes at a time.

I explained: "Jack, when you are going to do this exercise you need to make it a special time. You must prepare for your visualization. Find a place that is quiet where you will not be interrupted and sit with your spine straight, your feet flat on the floor, and your hands in your lap.

"I want you to relax your whole body. You may do this by deep breathing. When you are ready, begin by taking a deep breath on four counts, hold the breath for four counts, and release the breath on four counts. Do this three times."

I knew that Jack was a nervous wreck and that he had to relax before he could begin to have an added power to his focus. He repeated back to me the whole exercise. I then proceeded to explain the Divine Force. Jack had a Christian background and had no trouble understanding this spiritual concept. He left the session armed with his notes and a determined will that he would be faithful to practicing his role.

As he was leaving, I added this: "Jack, you must do everything humanly possible to help make this happen. It's no good to sit at home and wait for the phone to ring. You must do everything conceivable to accomplish your goal."

Four months after this session, Jack left a telephone message. He was overwhelmed because his mother sent him a check that paid all his credit card debt and left him with a few thousand extra dollars. He had no idea that his mother had extra money. She is a widow and he did not want to tell her about his problems because he feared it would worry her. She sent this money telling him she had been saving it to leave him when she died but somehow the thought of sending it now kept coming into her mind. And so she did. Jack sounded a little stunned about getting this money. Jack was on his way to an acting class that he paid for with some of the extra money from his mother. He was grateful to me for introducing him to thought. He was going to continue practicing thought control and he was now going to change his visualization and see himself in his new role, which was a working actor.

About eighteen months after the telephone call telling me about his mother's gift of the money, I received a note from Jack. He had gotten a part as a character actor in a TV crime show. His part was small but he would be seen on two episodes. He had been taking acting classes and gone to every possible open audition that he read about in the trades or heard about through conversations with other actors in class. He was relentless in his pursuit of his dream of being a working actor. He was still teaching and money was scarce but he was making ends meet. He knew that he would have to continue with his mental exercises and his physical labor but he was optimistic, which gave him added faith that he would continue to attract acting work and eventually make a living from artistic expression.

Deanne

Deanne was a single mother with two small children, living on welfare. She had a dream. She wanted a respectable profession, a good home, and money to educate her children. I have never met anyone with more moxie than Deanne. She met me at a book signing and told me her story. I happily had a few minutes to spend with her. I advised her to see herself working at a job that made her feel proud and useful. She should see herself in a nice home and waving to the kids as they go to school. I told her that she must *see this done.*

This woman amazed me with her absolute conviction that she would go home and immediately start these mental exercises. There was something about her that made me feel positive that she would achieve everything that she wished for. Three years later, Deanne came for an appointment. She had a job as a correction officer. She was living in a charming house and her kids were both doing well in school.

I asked her how she did this. She told me that not for one second did she ever let herself not completely believe that it would all be done. She was vigilant in seeing everything done. She met a woman who told her how to become a correction officer. This had never dawned on her before. She got the study material, worked hard, and passed with flying colors. She now had a steady job, so she qualified for a home mortgage. She found a home in an area where the public schools were great. She wanted to see me to tell me how much the advice at the book signing had helped to change her life.

Jimmy

Jimmy could not decide what he wanted to do when he grew up. He went to college, studied business, dropped out, went back to college, studied law, and dropped out again. He then decided he would study psychology, but he didn't like it. So he quit. It became evident that college was not for him. But what could he do? He loved to cook for his friends so why not become a chef? He enrolled at the Culinary Institute of America in New York and after three months decided that cooking as a profession was harder than he had imagined. Once again he dropped the course. When he came to see me, he was working as a bartender. He had taken the job because he had to pay his bills. He hated being a bartender and felt it was beneath him. Jimmy could not stand the customers but had to be cordial so he would not be fired. Hopefully, I could help him to decide what he wanted to do with his life.

I cautioned Jimmy about his negative thinking. His aura showed me that he was angry and frustrated. His state of mind was more detrimental than he realized. I could also tell as I looked at him that he was by nature a kind and loving man. The frustration of trying to find meaningful work had taken its toll. Jimmy listened intently.

"Just tell me what to do and I will do it."

Mental Exercise

I told Jimmy that he had to see himself happy at work. Because he did not know what this would entail, I told him to leave all his options open. He needed to allow the Divine Force to guide him to the perfect job. I instructed him to sit in a quiet, comfortable place and after asking the Divine Force to guide him he should see a picture in his mind of himself going to a place of work looking very upbeat and happy. He should see what he is wearing, see the way he is walking, and see himself being happy as he writes checks to pay his bills. The picture should be made as clear as he possibly can. He should do this at least three times a day, for at least two minutes each time.

He would discover that as he began to enjoy the process of creating a picture of himself happy in his work, he would feel like holding this picture longer. He would find that details would begin to be added to the picture. He should see what type of car he would drive to work and the physical surroundings at the workplace. He had gone to college, studied law and psychology, and was interested in being a chef. When he finished this exercise, he should release the picture and go on with his day. It is very important that he lets the picture go so his mind is free to receive other ideas that will lead him to his desired goal.

When we hold a picture, we are concentrating all of our thought on one specific image. This is fine, but it may limit his ability to receive ideas he never thought about. He must have faith that the answer will come. He must not vacillate and he has to persist with this mental exercise until he gets the answer he is looking for. It may take discipline because he is not used to doing this. But I believed that in a short time he would begin to enjoy these visualizations, so integration would replace discipline.

When we are integrated, we don't feel put upon by the demands to practice. For example, if you want to learn to play the piano you have to practice. If you persist and keep yourself thinking about how lovely it will be when you can play a nice melody with ease, the process becomes tolerable. As you become more proficient, you will find yourself looking forward to these practice sessions. You will no longer need to use force because you have become integrated. Integration means that you are happy to do whatever it takes in order to achieve the desired results. It is a constructive state of thinking.

Jimmy did what I told him. He found himself enjoying his moments of visualizations. It was not only relaxing but set the tone for his day. He was doing something that made him feel he was moving toward his goal. He did not feel alone because he felt connected to the Divine Force. He found it was much easier to go to his job at the bar and be nice to people. He did not feel resentment anymore and started to enjoy talking to his customers. His friends noticed that he seemed happier and commented on it. Six months passed. He was at work when one of his regular clients, Bill, introduced him to a friend named Mark, who was the personal assistant of a famous movie director. Jimmy found this interesting because he was fascinated with movie people. They talked and it turned out that Mark knew of a famous actor who was looking for a new assistant.

Jimmy said, "That sounds like an interesting job."

"Would you like to interview for this position? I can arrange that," Mark said.

Jimmy was a little surprised and added: "You don't even know me. How can you refer me?"

Bill piped in, "I will vouch for you, anytime."

"That's good enough for me," was Mark's reply.

Jimmy gave Mark his phone number, not necessar-

ily expecting to hear from him. He forgot about it. A week went by, the phone rang, and the voice asked, "Hi, Jimmy, this is Mark, remember me?" It took Jimmy a second to remember and then he said, "Of course, I do, you are a friend of Bill's."

"If you want to interview for the job I told you about, you have to come here right now." Mark explained that this actor was in town between movies and had time to meet with Jimmy.

"Tell me where to go and I will be there," Jimmy replied.

Jimmy got the job.

He came to see me a month after he started the new job. His background in law and psychology (and even cooking) came in very helpful, as he had to handle complicated situations for this famous person. He told me he loved the job and felt like he had found his calling. The job involved travel, meeting interesting people, and the pay was great. He even got a car. He had an office in New York and Los Angeles. Jimmy thanked me for my guidance.

"I would have never gotten this if I had not learned how to focus my thinking. It is amazing to see how this works. When I left the session with you, I was skeptical. It seemed impossible that I could discover my calling by visualizing myself happy three times a day. But I decided to give it a try. Nothing else had helped me. I have never been particularly spiritual, so using the Divine Force was not natural for me. I now cannot imagine starting my day without acknowledging this Force. I am so grateful."

■

Jimmy made a good point when he said it seemed too easy just to spend time picturing himself happy at work. Most people think they must be doing something more active in order to achieve the kind of result that Jimmy obtained. The mental exercise is the most important activity that we can do. But we must do whatever we can to make our picture a reality in our physical world. When Jimmy stopped hating his job, he was happier and more interested in listening and talking to his customers. This made Mark want to talk to him. The conversation they shared resulted in leading Jimmy to this perfect job.

This mental exercise worked for Jimmy. It can work for anyone who is unhappy with their work. No one needs to live without fulfilling work. It may take courage to focus your thought on a completely different career. It may take time. It could take a change of residence or a change of lifestyle. But many people have successfully made job or career changes. These people kept seeing the picture of themselves happy at work. They did whatever they had to do in order to make this happen. They kept the faith and did not give up. They followed the rules of thought.

■ 5. TRUE LOVE

Too often people who have a great deal of sexual attraction believe they are in love. Sexual attraction can be a potent elixir. It has a magnetic pull. When you add having things in common, such as travel, fine dining, and summers at the beach, they believe their love will last forever. Time passes and the sexual attraction dies down. Their common interests become mundane. They feel they have fallen out of love. These people were never in love in the first place. It wasn't love, it was attraction. This attraction was not strong enough to penetrate into the soul. So it died.

In the early stages of these types of relationships, people's thoughts are in sync. They vibrate at the same rate. These vibrations keep the relationship connected for a certain period. But then the vibrations are weak-

247

ened by interferences from other more powerful thought vibrations. For example, one of these two people becomes sexually attracted to someone else. Then they find out that the things they had in common were not strong enough to keep them together. They were no longer on the same wavelength. They were vibrating differently.

Sexual attraction and common interests are important. But they are not enough. They are solely physical. It is all material. It does not penetrate into the soul. When two people love each other on a soul level, it lasts. The qualities of the soul are connected to our higher self. These qualities are integrity, honesty, patience, courtesy, kindness, compassion, understanding, and tolerance. The sum total of all of these qualities makes an individual's character. Your character is your soul. Like attracts like. When two people of like-minded character come together, it results in a lasting connection. It is a merging of their souls. It goes beyond the physical and material constraints. When they love, it is true love.

To find true love, you must begin by being a loving person. That force of love creates a beautiful vibration that permeates your total being. This vibration will attract a similar person into your life.

If you want true love, you must focus your mind on true love. The act of concentrating on love puts you in the right frame of mind. This frame of mind prepares you for visualizing your true love. When you focus on love with a sincere desire to love and be loved, you will bring love into your life. Things reflect in kind. The more often you can discipline your mind to meditate on love the faster your individual desire will be brought into your physical life. There are many ways that we can focus on love.

Rose Exercise

Here is an effective way to focus on love. Sit in a quiet place. Make sure you are comfortable. Close your eyes. See the color "rose," a beautiful shade of pink. Keep your mind on this color. Do not fear if your mind strays. Just bring it back to the color "rose." Keep seeing the color. Breathe. Now see this beautiful color surrounding you. You are enveloped in a blanket of rose. Your aura emanates this beautiful color of love. You are feeling warm, protected, and loving. Hold this image for several minutes. Don't despair if you cannot hold it. It takes practice. Now send this color to someone who needs it. Anyone, it could be your mother, your boss, your neighbor, or someone who works in the corner deli who is always in bad temper. Just see the person who needs this love and see them enveloped in this beautiful pink. Hold this image until they are immersed in loving pink. Then let the image go.

You will be amazed by the results of this meditation. First of all, you will feel good. It is impossible not to be affected by a sincere focus on love. Second, you are selflessly sending love to someone because they need it, not because you want something. This action elevates all of your thoughts. We know that things reflect in kind. It will soon be obvious that love brings back love.

To find true love
begin by being
a loving person

Jessica and Philip

Jessica has been divorced for three years. She was feeling that the one thing she wanted more than anything else in her life was true love. She had tried very hard to make her marriage work, but she and her ex-husband were incompatible. Jessica felt that time was passing by and she feared that her dream would never become reality.

"I am not even dating. I don't know anybody whom I could see myself married to."

I said, "Jessica, that doesn't matter. You will attract a person into your life if you keep your mind open and your thoughts focused on true love."

"How do I focus on true love?"

"Like attracts like. You must be a person capable of true love in order to bring a person into your life who will truly love you."

I gave her the "rose exercise." This would help her to feel more loving. Then I went on to explain to her how to visualize her desire. I told her to prepare herself for this exercise. She must find a quiet, comfortable place where she will not be interrupted. I also told her to relax her body by deep breathing and when relaxed she should see a blank screen come down in front of her. She should begin to create a picture of herself with a person she is truly in love with. She could create this picture however it would work for her. Some people see their wedding; others see themselves hand in hand walking along the beach at sunset.

Jessica told me that her picture of true love was being in front of a fireplace drinking wine with the man of her dreams.

"That's fine," I said, "the more details you can put in your picture the better. See what you are wearing by the fire. See what the room looks like."

Jessica said she always loved creating stories. She would not have any trouble creating this picture. I also suggested that Mozart's music could be very helpful. It would make her feel peaceful and harmonious. This feeling could stay with her and would make her more receptive to people who were also harmonious. She had no problem with this. She loved Mozart.

"Jessica," I said, "you have to do everything in your power to attract this person into your life. You will have to make an effort to go to places that will make it easier to meet men. Patience is necessary and persistence is paramount."

"I wish I had more faith," she sighed.

"The fact that you wish you had more faith is a start

toward getting more. A positive attitude helps a great deal. Have faith in the possibility that by changing your thinking you can change your life. This type of thought will assist you."

Jessica started that very day. She chose a beautiful corner in her apartment to do her visualizations. She bought some Mozart music and had it set to play her chosen pieces. Jessica enjoyed these sessions because they were relaxing and interesting. She kept adding more and more details to her picture by the fireplace. The exercise for sending "love" made her feel good. Jessica did this religiously for close to a year. She met a number of eligible men during that time. No one clicked. In the old days, she would have gotten frustrated and cynical but she remained focused.

One afternoon, Jessica was on her way home and it began to rain. She was getting soaked. Having no umbrella she tried to hail a taxi. Almost like a miracle, one stopped right in front of her. This is no small feat in New York City on a rainy afternoon. As she started to get into the taxi, a man went for the cab at the same moment. He backed off, and Jessica heard herself saying, "Where are you going?" They happened to be going in the same direction. They shared the taxi. She had not even looked at him. The rest is history.

Jessica and Philip love telling the story of how they met, got to know each other, and realized that they were deeply in love. They had their honeymoon in a beautiful Vermont inn. This inn was known for having lovely rooms with large fireplaces. They have been married for five years. I think that what is good for them now will only get better with time.

Charles

Charles never threw anything away. Ten years before our meeting he'd read an article about me in a magazine. The article talked about my work and gave my office phone number. Charles had kept this, believing he would call for an appointment when the time was right. He was looking for something in his basement and there, among the papers that had been gathered for years, was the article with my phone number. At this moment, Charles was in a bad state. His wife of sixteen years had left him and he was devastated. He called and made the appointment.

Charles arrived so upset that his hands were trembling. I got him a glass of water. He thanked me, and tears began to trickle down his cheeks.

"It will be all right, Charles," I said as I sat down. I

gave him a minute to calm himself. Many times people cry during a session with me. But it's rare to have a man break down before we get started.

"My wife has left me." He could barely get the words out.

"She will be back," I said with a definiteness that made him stop crying.

"You don't get it. She is in love with somebody else," he interjected.

"She thinks she is," I said.

"What do you mean?" he asked.

"It isn't love, it is sexual attraction. When the attraction dies, she will come back."

"Are you sure?"

I told him what I saw. "Your wife fell for an artist. She wants to believe that she is his muse. She believes he is a passionate, loving man who will worship her. She will discover that he is selfish, crude, and neglectful, and he isn't even a good artist."

Charles was stunned. He had never talked to a psychic and hadn't expected me to be able to know that much. But I could see that my words gave him faith.

"Do you think you can forgive her?" I asked.

"I love her. I will do anything to have her back. I want another chance to make her happy."

"You'll have to be very patient. She is in the throes of passion. It won't do any good to try to convince her to come back right now."

"All my friends say that I am fooling myself. She won't be back. They think I'm crazy to want her back at all."

"Well, they don't understand how much the two of you truly love each other."

"The two of us? Do you think she loves me?"

"Yes. I see that she loves you deeply. She has let herself make a bad choice. I think she was unhappy with her own work. She sought something exciting and so she ran off."

"She always wanted to be an artist. I told her that I'd support her if she wanted to pursue art. But she didn't believe she had enough talent."

Charles was not handsome, but his kindness and loving nature made him very appealing. I had rarely met anyone who loved with his degree of selflessness. He wasn't judging his wife even though he was heartbroken. He wanted the opportunity to love her more.

"How long do you think it will take before she wants to come home?" he asked.

"That depends a lot on you," I answered. "You need

to send your wife loving thoughts. You must not allow your thoughts to go negative. You will have trouble keeping the faith that she is coming back to you. Your friends won't help. I would not talk to them about this. Keep a clear picture in your mind seeing the two of you back together." I added that he should spend some time getting the house in better order.

Charles admitted that his wife hated his inability to throw things away. He promised to spend time eliminating clutter. This would also keep his mind occupied and help him to be less lonely.

"Just act as if she is on a vacation," I said.

"What a good way to think about this," he added.

Charles left the session feeling much better, but knew that the wait would not be easy. But I also saw the real love that these two felt for each other. She would find that she did not love the artist. Charles's right thinking would help his wife come to this conclusion sooner than later. His thoughts could be transmitted to her. These powerful thoughts would help her to forgive herself for her bad judgment.

Charles came back to see me three years later. True love prevailed. His wife had come back six months earlier. Shortly after she'd left Charles, she knew she'd made a terrible mistake. The artist was a mean-spirited loser. He treated her badly. It did not take long to realize that it wasn't love that they shared. She was ashamed of herself and realized she loved Charles. It took time for her to have the nerve to see if he would take her back. She told him that many times she could feel him thinking about her. Sometimes the thought would be so strong she would feel as if she'd been with Charles. This gave her courage to contact him. And finally they were reunited.

Telepathy

Thought isn't bound by the laws of physical matter. If we concentrate our thought on a person and the person we are thinking about is receptive, our thought can be picked up in their mind. Charles thought about his wife so often and so intently that she picked up on this. His thoughts had been transferred to his wife. This is telepathy. Have you ever thought about someone and the phone rang and it was that person on the line? Have you ever run into someone whom you just thought or spoke about? Have you ever gone to the mailbox and received a letter from someone who had just been on your mind? I have found that telepathy between people who truly love each other is most common. Because these two are so connected, their thoughts about each other are intensely magnetized. This increased magnetism gives the thoughts added force and makes them easier to be received.

True love is possible. It is easier to find it if we focus our thoughts on becoming a loving person. We should visualize ourselves happy in love. This type of picture sets a tone that vibrates with harmony. When we are in harmony, it is easier to follow the rules of thinking. Following the rules will result in finding the true love that we are all seeking.

■ 6. HAPPINESS

Happiness is living in harmony. Harmony is the universal law of equilibrium. Everything good is contained in harmony. Health, balance, love, friendship, and happiness are the result of living in harmony. All problems such as illness, despair, loneliness, and emptiness are the result of living in disharmony.

Harmony means that you are at peace with your inner self and your external world at the same time. When we think, speak, and act in harmony we send balanced, positive vibrations out into the ether. These vibrations emit harmonious impulses that possess a magnetic force. This magnetic force draws like-minded people and things to us. The greater the positive magnetic force the greater harmony is created in our lives.

Many people are unhappy. A great number of people believe that they would be happy with their lives if they just had more money. If they could only win the lottery, receive an inheritance, or get an excellent paying job, everything would be fine. There is nothing innately wrong with having money or beautiful things. Money alone, however, does not guarantee happiness.

There are many stories about lottery winners who turn out to be losers. They end up divorced, broke, in debt, or in rehab. Haven't you read the numerous stories about siblings who sue each after their parents died? They felt they have been short-changed in their inheritance. Then there are the battles of family members to gain control of assets while the parents are still alive. As a result of these battles over money, siblings often never speak to each other again.

Everyone wants to be happy. People make us happy, not things. It is relationships that produce happiness in our lives.

Edward

Edward, a wealthy, handsome businessman was depressed. He was a man who seemed to be at the end of his rope. The odd thing was that there did not appear anything around him that would immediately explain the depths of his despair. My first impulse was to suggest that he talk to a psychiatrist and not to a psychic. It can be difficult to work with people who are really depressed because it is hard to read through a veil of gloom. But as Edward spoke to me, I could see that he was not really depressed. He was just desperately unhappy. He told me that he had come to see me because there was nothing he enjoyed anymore or that made him happy. He asked me what he could do to find happiness.

Edward had traveled the world. There was almost nowhere he had not been. He had made a fortune in business and had just married a beautiful, intelligent, much younger woman. He thought having a family might make him happy at this stage of his life.

Edward had done everything. He learned how to fly an airplane and had gone big-game hunting. He raced boats, skied, and played tennis like a professional. Everything Edward wanted to do he did. After he had accomplished something he felt content for a short time, maybe

a few months. Then he was compelled to try to find some-thing to do that was more exciting and challenging.

He was obsessed with his own unhappiness. He told an acquaintance about his unhappiness and this man suggested that Edward set up a charity. "That will make you feel good," he told Edward.

Edward thought it through and decided to donate money to his alma mater. He donated a large sum. This bought the school a new building, upon which Edward's name appeared. This made him feel good for a little longer than usual. But soon he was back to searching for happiness.

As I watched Edward and listened to him, I could see that he was completely narcissistic and self-centered. It was all about him. Even the charity was about him and his name. It had nothing to do with sincere generosity. When I pointed this out to him, he looked at me in shock.

"What do you mean by self-centered? I gave two million to my alma mater. I let my wife buy anything she wants. I take everyone out to dinner. I always pay. What's selfish about that?"

"Edward, you are completely motivated by doing something that makes you feel good, not because you are doing something for someone else. I have never heard you say one thing about friendships, relationships, or love. You cannot find happiness unless you learn how to think about the needs of other people, not just your own. When you speak of your wife, all you talk about is the money that you provide her with. What about how she feels about your life together?"

I could see another divorce in his future. His wife needed to have a relationship with her husband, not just a huge bank account. I stressed that relationships, not money alone, make people happy. In order to be happy, Edward needed to change the way he thought about and related to people. Loving people makes you happy, and even happier than that is loving people with no ulterior motive. But that would be a lot for Edward to try to digest. Maybe his extraordinary unhappiness would force him to at least attempt to examine his thinking. He'd discover through this self-examination that he needed to make changes in his thinking. He was a man who liked challenges. So I decided to give him one. I told him that for the next forty-eight hours he must not allow himself to hold a negative thought.

"What do you mean by negative thought?" he asked me.

"Any thought of failure; any thought of criticism, spite, or jealousy; any unkind thought; any thought of sickness, accident, or trouble. In short, any thought that is pessimistic or not constructive is a negative thought."

Then I told him, "Negative thoughts will come to your mind but you must not dwell on them. It does not matter what thought comes into your mind as long as you don't entertain the thought. The moment a negative thought comes into your mind you must replace it with a positive one. When you dwell or hold on to a thought, a strong form is created. If you release the thought quickly, it cannot produce a lasting form. You must stop thinking you are unhappy and replace this thought with a kind, productive, or constructive one. This will take an extraordinary mental discipline. In fact, I am not sure if you can do it."

"Yes, I can do that."

"Okay, Edward, give it a try."

I continued, "Edward, think about this before you start your forty-eight hours. It is very difficult to do this exercise. If you make a mistake or fall backward, you must start again at the beginning. You must not get mad at yourself or feel like a failure, just start again. The clock will again be ticking. You must continue this exercise until you are able to keep your mind completely focused on positive thoughts for forty-eight hours. I will expect to hear from you when you have been able to do this."

Edward left the session believing that this was a piece of cake.

"How much do you want to bet that I will call you in forty-eight hours?" he asked.

I laughed and said, "It's still about money, Edward, isn't it? Just keep in mind, I am a psychic and I will know whether or not you have really done this."

Two years passed and I had forgotten about Edward. I thought I would never hear from him again. But he came for another appointment. His second marriage had ended. Edward's wife had left him. She told him that she could not live with someone who was so insensitive. She needed someone she could talk to and who tried to understand her. This made Edward finally realize that I had been right.

He told me, "After I had left the first session, I had started the mental exercise that you had given me. I decided it was silly. What does thinking have to do with anything? A man needs to do something."

Now, Edward felt, maybe he did need to examine his thinking and change the way he related to people. This time I knew Edward would make a sincere effort to observe the way he thought, spoke, and acted. He was an intelligent man and did have discipline, if he wanted to achieve something.

One month passed and Edward called me. He was as excited as a child with a new puppy. He told me that he had made five attempts to get through forty-eight hours, but could not do it. When he failed, he would take a few days to get his mental strength built up, then he would try again. On his sixth attempt, he finally believed that he was successful. He wanted to make an appointment with me so that I could verify this. And I did. Edward had done it. Hopefully, this would start him on a new habit of thinking. Edward was happy about his achievement and he seemed determined to keep it up.

We must focus our thoughts on harmony. Happiness comes from living in harmony. Visualize happiness. Don't falter. Have faith. Persist. The Divine Force is always available to help us. We promote harmony by thinking about others. I have never met a happy selfish person. Our thoughts are like keys on the piano. Some musical notes played together produce harmony. Others will bring discord. Thought is energy and vibration. The rate of vibration of your thoughts will cause you to attract things that vibrate at the same rate. That is why you hear that you must be a good friend in order to have good friends. You must love in order to be loved. Happiness draws happiness to itself.

*e*very conception is an
immaculate conception.
We cannot
conceive a soul.

six

ONLY THE
SOUL SURVIVES

*T*he soul is the sum total of our thoughts. It is our character. The physical body dies but the soul does not. Thoughts do not die. They live in the soul. The soul lives on after physical death.

In order to understand the soul, it is important to think of ourselves as having two bodies: a physical body and an etheric body. The etheric body is often called the spirit body. This body is composed of a much finer substance than the physical body. When we die, the etheric body is severed from the physical body.

There is a silver cord that connects the physical and etheric bodies together. This cord, like your aura, has a color and can be seen by people who have a psychic gift. At the moment of death, this cord breaks. In a near-death experience, the cord is not severed and remains intact. The etheric body releases partially from the physical body, but the physical and the etheric bodies remain connected. Reports of near-death experiences come from people who were clinically dead but were resuscitated and brought back to life. For example, people that were on the operating table who report feeling as if they were floating above their physical body. Outside their body, yet still in the physical realm, they could see themselves lying on the operating table. They watched themselves being brought back to life. They heard the voices of the doctors and nurses and they saw the steps it took to bring them back to physical life. Next, they felt as if they were going through a tunnel. At the end of the tunnel they saw a bright light. Before they reached the light they saw their lives pass before them. Then they heard a voice in their head of someone whom they knew had already died before them. "It's not your time yet. There are things for you to do in the physical world."

Almost everyone who has had a near-death experience returns to the physical body quickly. Near-death experiences do not occur only on the operating table, but also during heart attacks, in near-drowning accidents, or with hypothermia and in choking situations. Invariably, you hear that no one wanted to go back to earth life. They all wanted to stay in the spirit world. Don't you find this interesting if death supposedly is so frightening? Why do people who have glimpsed the spirit world tell us that the experience was wonderful? They reported an enhanced appreciation for the power of thought because they had glimpsed the afterlife, which is the world of thought. They said that they felt incredible security and peace while they were out of their physical body. They also felt a new understanding for the sacredness of life. They realized that the purpose of life on earth is to learn, to improve, and to help others.

All these people in near-death situations experienced life in the etheric body. The etheric body interpenetrates the physical body and is attached to it with a silver cord. As long as the silver cord is still connected to the physical body, the person is physically alive. Think about it as a kite. It can fly high. It can move quite a distance from the hand holding the string. Sometimes the etheric body loosens from the physical body and moves away, it flies out of sight. But, like the kite, the etheric body can be brought back as long as it stays connected.

When we physically die, the cord breaks and we are free of the physical body. In virtually all cases, we are as

unconscious of dying as we are of falling asleep. Death is like taking off a glove. The instant preceding death, we review all the events of the life that has just finished. Simply, we see our lives pass before us. This happens quickly and appears like moving pictures flashed on the screen of the mind.

This process of review is very important. We are made aware of all the successes and failures and of all our thoughts, words, and actions in the life just lived. With this knowledge fresh in our memory, we enter into the afterlife. The soul passes over and awakens in the spirit world. This new world is sometimes a bit confusing. In all cases, a friend or relative who has passed on before welcomes us to this new realm. Our souls go to the kind of place that we have prepared by our thinking and living on the earth. All the conditions of the physical world are the results of our thoughts. The exact same thing is true of the afterlife. We earn our place in the afterlife by how we lived in this life. We live in the spirit world until the time when the soul returns to the physical world. When the soul returns it will enter an appropriate physical body to facilitate its development. We create a body, not a soul. That is why every conception is an immaculate conception. We cannot conceive a soul.

Have you ever wondered why there are such differences between people? Why one person is born into a nice family with wealth and position and another into a broken home with poverty and neglect? Why is one person born with perfect physical health and another born with some horrible disease? Why are there such differences in talents?

The answer is that this life we are living is not our only life. We have lived many lives. We have thought, said, and done lots of things, good and bad. We are reaping today the results of not only our current thoughts and actions but our prior ones as well. The Bible says, "Whatsoever a man soweth, that shall he also reap." This is the law of cause and effect. We are born into the life we have earned by our actions. We can be happy in the future if we begin now to think and act with love and service to others. It does not matter what mistakes we have made in the past, we can start at this moment to create a better future.

The soul is born into the physical world to learn certain lessons. The soul is a depository that holds all our thoughts, actions, and experiences. This is our personality. When we die, we cast off the physical body but we take the etheric (soul-body) with us into the afterlife.

The soul holds the memory of every experience we have had. The soul, like an actor in a repertory company, plays many roles. These roles afford us different opportunities for growth. We should do everything we can to become more tolerant, more loving, and more selfless people. These qualities are acquired through directing our thoughts and actions in a positive, productive, and kind manner. This type of thinking elevates the soul. The more we elevate our soul the better we are able to attract good things into our lives. We attract everything in this life and the next one by our thinking. It is always good to be guided by the knowledge, only the soul survives.

■ MAKEOVERS

The world is obsessed with makeovers. Magazines, television, newspapers, blogs, and coffee shop conversations are consumed with makeover madness. There are Botox, silicone, laser surgery, tummy-, chin-, butt-tucks, and whatever else can be tucked, stomach bypasses, eye jobs, nose jobs, breast reductions, breast enhancements, hair removal, and hair transplants. You can cut your hair, add hair pieces, change your hair color, wax your eyebrows, and don't forget your teeth. Teeth can be whitened, capped, transplanted, or straightened in order to create the perfect mouth that reflects the current trend, ultimately producing the smile that can be compared to the movie star du jour. One of my clients proudly announced that she was going to have her teeth fixed in order to have her mouth look like Julia Roberts. Another client was so obsessed with having her face made over that she had plastic surgery eleven times. She is still unhappy with the results.

You can put your picture on a computer and see how you would look ten or twenty years from now if you do not do anything. The normal process of aging terrorizes people. Many are sold on the fantasy that the more they alter their physical appearance the more likely they will reverse the aging process.

A well-known client of mine was so obsessed about her age that she somehow got her driver's license, passport, and even her birth certificate altered. She lived in the terror that people would find out how old she really was. On her deathbed she refused to have her obituary written as she feared someone she went to school with would read it and tell the truth about her age. There was a one-line notice about her death in the *New York Times.* Her age was not listed.

Janice

Janice arrived for her session with me in hysteria. She cried nonstop through the whole session. She was going to celebrate her fortieth birthday and was inconsolable. Every time I tried to say something of comfort, her sobs got louder and louder.

Janice had been a famous rock disc jockey and she believed that being forty was death in her business. I pointed out the radio personalities and rock stars, who were not only past forty but in their fifties and sixties, still going strong.

Janice did not want to hear that. She just kept saying she could not live with the fact that she was getting older. She had started injections and plastic surgery procedures while she was in her thirties. She believed the earlier one started it the better they worked. She was dieting to the point of malnutrition and wore clothes that were pictured in teen fashion magazines. She looked unbalanced.

Janice came to see me four times within a five-year period. I tried to help her focus her thinking on the good things in her life. She refused to see anything positive as she continued her obsessive thinking about the horror of getting older.

During our last session I pleaded with her, "Janice, if you don't stop this negative, obsessive thinking something will happen that will indeed shorten your life."

Janice died of cancer at the age of forty-six. She would never have to be old. What a heartbreak.

Janice is a frightening example of the power that our thoughts have on our lives. She repeated over and over, day after day, year after year, "I cannot bear getting older." She kept her mind completely focused on her anger and fear about the normal aging process. There is an old saying: "Be careful of what you wish for, as you may get it."

Janice did not consciously think about dying but her thinking made her sick. I have seen hundreds of people over the years in various states of upset over getting older. Most of them are not as extreme as Janice, but their anxiety always results in some type of action. Buying sports cars, lifting the hems of skirts, taken on younger lovers are a few examples of what people believe will make them feel and seem younger. These are temporary fixes that ultimately leave people feeling unhappy. Because the reality remains—everyone gets older.

277

Aging is not the only reason for the pursuit of transformation. The desire to transform the physical body has become to many people the center of their universe. The pursuit of the perfect body has resulted in a world where eating disorders have reached epidemic proportions, most of these being rooted in the desire to look like the models and movie stars that grace the magazine covers. It is not only the physical body that is being obsessively made over, but it is your house, your wardrobe, your yard, your finances, your closets, and even the way you raise your children. People are trying to make over every part of their lives. All these makeovers are temporary and will make one feel better for a short period of time. Why has no one thought to make over the soul?

The other evening, I was watching a talk show. A famous spokeswoman from one of the diet programs was a guest. She said she had lost fifty pounds, had her kinky hair straightened, cleared up her debts, and worked hard on "loving herself." Yet, it had been two years since she had been asked out on a date. She said that she felt better about herself but was perplexed. She did not understand why men weren't flocking to her.

Meanwhile, she talked about nothing good. She

talked critically of all her past relationships, blaming everyone else for her troubles. This made me think about her makeover. Obviously, she didn't realize how self-centered she seemed. Everything this woman had talked about and done was completely directed toward the physical. I did not hear her say a word about the soul. It was a pity that she did not realize how effective a soul makeover can be. If she had done this, she would have been busy loving others and not consumed with loving herself. She would have been busy focusing her thoughts on becoming a kinder, more tolerant person.

The vibration of selfless love is a potent magnet for attracting love. I predict if she'd taken time to change her thinking from the body to the soul, she would by now have a happy love life.

There is absolutely nothing wrong with carrying your soul in an attractive physical body clothed in elegant garments. It's good to enjoy a beautiful home with a lovely garden. But the lack of satisfaction that people seem to get of a permanent nature from all these makeovers proves that they are only superficial changes.

All of these makeovers are only touching the external parts of our lives. That is why they leave people feeling like there is something missing. Everything in life is temporary except for the soul. The soul is eternal. When we focus our thinking on transforming the qualities and parts of ourselves that are directly related to our soul, we will have immediate, amazing, and lasting results. This would be the ultimate makeover.

Remember thought is energy. This new thought is connected to the higher part of ourselves and sends out a purer energy. We will attract better jobs, resulting in greater security; better bodies, resulting in greater health, and, most of all, better character, resulting in more harmonious personal love relationships.

You may be thinking, "What do you mean by soul? I have never even seen a soul. How do I make over my soul?"

The soul is the part of us that does not die. The soul is a depository that holds all our thoughts, actions, and experiences. When we die, we cast off the physical body but we take the soul-body with us into the afterlife. The soul is a synthesis of all our lives.

We are born into the material world in order to master ourselves. Self-mastery is completed when we have gained complete control of our thought. Everything that requires mastery—be it health, finances, sex, emotions, relationships, work, or overall harmony—is done by raising our consciousness. In order to do this, we must undertake the earnest study of the power of thought. All transformation is a result of a conscious change in our thinking. This means that we must train ourselves to select and control our thoughts. The soul seeks freedom from the prison of negative thinking. Any thought that is not positive, constructive, and kind is negative. The soul reflects our thoughts. Nothing said or done by anyone else can disturb the process of raising the level of our thinking. It is only the reaction we have to the thinking of others that can affect us.

The soul is composed of our thoughts. Any change in our thinking immediately affects the soul. This may be positive or negative. In the physical world, our soul can be seen through our character. Character is the sum total of our thoughts. Good character traits are integrity, honesty, fairness, kindness, compassion, discipline, consideration, generosity, moderation, understanding, discernment, and love. These are qualities of the soul. Every time we improve any part of our character, we enhance our soul. The more we enhance our souls, the better our lives become.

When we focus our thinking on the Divine Force, we immediately elevate ourselves. We think within the higher part of our mind. The mind is dual. It is physical and metaphysical. Any makeovers that are related to our physical existence can only reap short-term bene-

fits, because the physical world dies. Nothing lasts. Your house does not stand forever. Your gardens will go to seed. Your children will grow up and leave. The physical body will die.

Any makeover that is related to the soul will reap permanent benefits, because the soul survives. It is eternal. It is the divine part of us. This is a God in embryo. We are born upon this earth in order to move toward mastering ourselves. We are given a body to facilitate this. The physical body is consumed with the desires of the material world.

People are terrified of getting old. Yet, when they comment on someone being an "old soul," they think this is someone who is wiser, more developed, and more beautiful. The truth is, older is not always wiser. Some people are born upon the earth over and over doing the very same things, never lifting themselves above the mass mind. Others grow more quickly. Thus, they are young souls needing greater spiritual and character development. The world is a schoolroom for our soul's education. We are born into circumstances that we have earned through our prior actions. Doesn't it make sense that we would aspire to become more spiritual people?

The only way to become a finer soul is through elevating our thinking. That is the only way we can become truly happy, and we all want to be happy. To think within the higher mind is wonderful. This type of thought emits a powerful energy that works like magic. As we learn to think this way, we begin to crave different experiences. We desire to be of greater service. Harmony becomes our main goal. Love and patience are the norm.

It is our will that we must strengthen in order to learn to think with our higher mind. The first step in learning to think in our higher mind is focus. We must focus our thoughts on subjects that enhance the soul. Any thought, word, or action that promotes harmony enhances the soul. It takes a determined will to keep our thought focused this way. After we are able to focus, we must then direct the thought in a manner that vibrates with kindness, patience, and love. We can find it very interesting to observe our thinking. We acquire a new habit of thinking, and we feel kinder and more loving. These soul qualities make everything easier. Our needs and desires are manifested with greater ease than we ever thought was possible.

You create a body and the soul enters. You cannot see the soul, just like you cannot see a thought. You can see the actions that reflect the development of the soul.

The soul vibrates with a certain amount of light. This is seen in the aura. Every time we overcome an obstacle such as an addiction to drugs, a tendency toward revenge, greed, or hatred in any form, the light that envelops our soul increases in intensity. Every time we can stay positive and constructive we raise the vibration of our soul. This increases the light that emanates from the soul's aura. The greater the light emanating from our soul, the finer the caliber of experience we are able to attract, for like always attracts like. Kindred souls are magnetically drawn together.

This is the secret of life: Everything begins and ends with thought.

We earn our place in the
next world by the way
we have lived
in this world

seven

THE AFTERLIFE

When we die, we take our thoughts with us. Thoughts do not die. The afterlife is the world of thought. This world is also known as the other side and the spirit world. This is where the etheric body, which is our soul body, goes when the physical body dies.

When the physical body dies, the soul remains. The physical body is merely a layer that is cast off, no longer necessary. When we cast off the physical body, the desires attached to the physical body are thrown off. It is no longer necessary to maintain the material world. We don't need to eat, sleep, work, make money, maintain property, or do anything connected to the physical existence. The soul now lives on a different plane, which is the world of thought.

We enter the afterlife when the review of the current life has ended, and the silver cord has broken. We will have our full memory in the afterlife. As we pass from this life to the next one, we fall into a sleeplike state. We awaken to find a friend or relative or many friends and relatives there to greet us. In the rare case that someone passes over without knowing anyone in the afterlife, helpers are waiting to welcome the arrival. No one enters the afterlife alone. The conditions of the life entered after death depends upon the type of life lived before death.

The moment we arrive in the spirit world the complete realization of the power of thought will be overwhelming. After we arrive in spirit, we'll immediately see the action of our thought. There is no delay. Thought and action happen simultaneously.

On earth we must think about doing something and then perform the physical action in order to put the thought to work. Let's say you want to build a house. You must have plans drawn up, hire a contractor, and make numerous decisions about all the details of the project. In the spirit world, you think about the house you want and you have it. Action and thought are instantaneous. This takes a little time to get used to. It's difficult to comprehend the power and force of our thought.

Clothing is made by thought in the afterlife. We

just think of ourselves as clothed and we become clothed. People dress in various styles. To think about clothes is to have them on. Many people choose to wear simple flowing robes. People gather together in thought-form houses and cities. The afterlife is just as varied as life on earth.

Thought is not visible in the physical world. In the afterlife, thought is completely visible when it is directed toward someone. Let's say you send a thought to your friend. It will appear to your friend as a flash of light and then they will hear the message in their mind. In the spirit world, thought has a higher vibration than it does on earth. That is why thought can be seen. In the afterlife, if we think we want to see someone we see them without delay.

When we die, we gravitate to the place where we belong. This is the place that we have prepared by our thinking, speaking, and actions on the earth plane. We are the same people in the spirit world that we were before death. The physical world is the schoolroom for our growth and development. It is in this world that we are educated. We learn from family relationships, schools, work, and friendships.

We grow from problem solving. We have to deal with physical problems. Our bodies need constant

attention. We get sick, become well, gain and lose weight, get tired, and build strength. The body is an extraordinary measurement for our overall well-being. The body reacts not only to the elements but to emotions and aging as well.

We must make a living. Money is necessary for physical existence. We are tested all the time by issues concerning money. One way our character is shown is by the way we handle money.

Every aspect of our life is completely determined by the way we think. Our thoughts guide our actions. We gain experience throughout our lives by the choices we make. Some people do not learn by experience. They make the same mistakes over and over. This limits their growth. All growth takes place while we live on earth. Every moment is an opportunity for our soul to grow. How we handle the good and the bad situations and events of our lives builds up our character.

When we die, we will go to a place in the spirit world that reflects the type of person we were at the end of our lives. You may have lived in poverty, ill health, lonely, or professionally disappointed, but you may live in beauty, health, and harmony in the afterlife. Your soul remains at the level of development it had reached just prior to your physical death. Every good thought produces positive energy. This energy is taken with you when you die.

Death does not enlighten anyone. During our life on earth, we have built our character. This makes up the type of person we are. A kind and loving person will reside in a beautiful part of the spirit world. We earn our place in the next world by the way we have lived in this world. In the spirit world, we will be drawn toward people who have similar interests and character. People with the same affinity and similar temperament are drawn together in spirit. The law of attraction, like attracts like, is in full operation.

A man who paints as a hobby who passes into spirit will remain interested in art. He will find other artists who painted in their spare time. They will enjoy exchanging ideas, techniques, and stories. He may have loved the paintings of Van Gogh or Gauguin, but he will not spend time with these great artists. These artists are busy painting and are surrounded by artists who have achieved the same degree of excellence. It is necessary to perfect your art in the physical world. You take your talent with you. It is the same amount of talent that you had prior to passing over. You may continue to enjoy the level of your expertise, but you will not enhance it in spirit.

Artists can inspire receptive people on earth. Their thoughts can be transferred from the spirit world to the earth. This is not easy. It takes great focus, energy, and deep concentration to achieve this. Inspiration is thought transference. There are many levels of inspiration that come from souls in the spirit world. We must remember that thought is vibration. It takes form. The form creates a picture. The picture is magnetized by energy. Thought can travel great distances faster than light. Thought is not restricted by physical laws. It is received instantaneously.

A businessman, who lived a life completely consumed by thoughts of his business, will think about his business in the afterlife. He will be drawn toward people with similar interests. Since there is no need to make money in the afterlife, he will discuss his successes and achievements with like-minded people. In time, he may start thinking about the things in his life he enjoyed that were not work oriented. He may have enjoyed spending time with his family or may have played bridge. But his main interest will remain his business.

A good doctor who passes over retains his medical knowledge in the spirit world. He will see the people who he helped while they were on the earth. There will be many wonderful encounters because the love and help he gave will be remembered.

A woman who had a family and lived her whole life in the same house in the same small town will re-create this in spirit. She will re-create her house and her personal belongings. She will be interested in talking to the family members and townsfolk who passed on as well. She will be happy living the same life in spirit that she did on earth.

The afterlife is a truly democratic place. Everyone has the right to live in a manner they choose. This right is earned by the life lived on earth.

People come to me asking if I can help them to communicate with the departed. They miss their loved ones and are desperate to know that they are safe and happy. Some people wrongly feel that all the departed can communicate at will.

There are misconceptions that reaching people in the afterlife is as simple as a phone call. It isn't. First, it is necessary to have a medium to send or receive messages. A medium is a channel for communication. One does not have to be a psychic to have mediumistic abilities. A medium is like a radio receiver. You must be able to pick up waves of thought. These waves have a certain magnetic energy. Mediums are usually born, not made. But there are cases where mediumship is acquired through study and certain mental exercises.

When people die, hopefully they let go of the physical world. But there are times when they don't. Some examples are unfinished business, strong physical desires, or death from a shock or accident. These occurrences can result in souls being earthbound. They are caught between the physical and the spirit worlds. When this happens, sightings as well as messages from them can occur. Ghosts are earthbound spirits. It is rare, but not impossible, that someone who does not have psychic gifts has seen a ghost. This would happen when a person was extremely tired or maybe ill. In those conditions, the astral body and the physical body are connected more loosely. This type of connection can leave one open to picking up thought not normally received. Mediumship is always a passive state. The body of the medium is used as a conduit.

Getting messages from the departed is possible, but it is better to let people rest in peace. If we are strongly grieving the dead, they can feel our sadness. We should send thoughts of love, not thoughts of loss. I know that it is difficult to say good-bye to our loved ones. But when we understand thought and its power it becomes easier to let go until we are all together in the afterlife. No matter how young someone dies it is only a short time until we will see them again. We do love beyond the grave. Thought does not die. We cannot see the departed. We cannot see their thoughts. But we can feel them.

There is nothing more powerful than thought. We create every aspect of our world through our thinking. We can change any part of our lives by learning the rules of thought and using them. There is nothing but thought.

Thought is everything. We are what we think.

ACKNOWLEDGMENTS

With gratitude to my editor, Malaika Adero, who is not only a superb editor but a graceful, passionate artist and friend who edited not only this book but also my first book, *Love in Action*.

Special thanks to Judith Curr, who supported the project from its inception. Judith creates an aura of harmony, love, and respect that makes everyone feel special for being part of Atria.

Additional thanks to Krishan Trotman and the team at Atria.

With appreciation to Jan Miller, who is an outstanding agent as well as a terrific friend. This is the fourth book that we have done together. Thanks also to her superb staff at Dupree Miller.

Thank you Rob Van Dorssen and Marja de Vries.

INDEX

R

Relaxation, breathing
    exercise for, 180
Resolutions, New Year's, 136
Right thinking, 45–47
Rose exercise, 250

S

Secret of life, 284
See it done, 125–137
  Mozart's music and, 176
Selfless motivation, role of,
    93
Sex, *See* Great sex
Soul
  defined, 269–274
  makeovers, 274–284
Speech
  careless, 59
  conflict, development of,
    54–55
  defined, 48–49
  emotions and, 61
  harmonious, 61, 63
  lies, 63–64

obscene, 57
observing, 188
power of, 48–65
preparing, 55–57
saying what you mean, 49–
  52
tone and, 50–51, 61
wasted, 59

T

Telepathy, 259–260
Telephone, support using,
    188–189
Tested, being, 194–197
Thought(s)
  See also The 5 Rules of
    Thought
  how they work, 16–22
  isolating, 184–185
  passing thought, 27
  learn to observe, 32–34
  reality and, 23–31
  using other people's,
    34–43
  vibration, 2–3, 28–29
  wave, 2